Job Interview

How To Succeed In An Interview By Beating Anxiety And Get A Job Of Your Dream

(Everything You Should Know To Be More Confident And Get The Job You Want)

Rudolph Norman

Published by Rob Miles

Rudolph Norman

All Rights Reserved

Job Interview: How To Succeed In An Interview By Beating Anxiety And Get A Job Of Your Dream (Everything You Should Know To Be More Confident And Get The Job You Want)

ISBN 978-1-989990-72-8

All rights reserved. No part of this guide may be reproduced in any form without permission in writing from the publisher except in the case of brief quotations embodied in critical articles or reviews.

Legal & Disclaimer

The information contained in this book is not designed to replace or take the place of any form of medicine or professional medical advice. The information in this book has been provided for educational and entertainment purposes only.

The information contained in this book has been compiled from sources deemed reliable, and it is accurate to the best of the Author's knowledge; however, the Author cannot guarantee its accuracy and validity and cannot be held liable for any errors or omissions. Changes are periodically made to this book. You must consult your doctor or get professional medical advice before using any of the suggested remedies, techniques, or information in this book.

Upon using the information contained in this book, you agree to hold harmless the Author from and against any damages, costs, and expenses, including any legal fees potentially resulting from the application of any of the information provided by this guide. This disclaimer applies to any damages or injury caused by the use and application, whether directly or indirectly, of any advice or information presented, whether for breach of contract, tort, negligence, personal injury, criminal intent, or under any other cause of action.

You agree to accept all risks of using the information presented inside this book. You need to consult a professional medical practitioner in order to ensure you are both able and healthy enough to participate in this program.

Table of Contents

INTRODUCTION 1

CHAPTER 1: WHAT ARE THE TYPES OF JOB INTERVIEWS? .. 6

CHAPTER 2: HOW TO PASS YOUR JOB INTERVIEW 10

CHAPTER 3: PREPARING TO ANSWER ANTICIPATED JOB INTERVIEW QUESTIONS 23

CHAPTER 4: TAKE CARE OF YOUR RESUME 34

CHAPTER 5: NETWORKING AND BUILDING PROFESSIONAL RELATIONSHIPS 39

CHAPTER 6: TAKING INVENTORY OF YOUR QUALIFICATIONS 49

CHAPTER 7: BUILDING A CONFIDENT RESUME 54

CHAPTER 8: HOW TO EXCEL IN AN INTERVIEW 59

CHAPTER 9: OTHER IMPORTANT TOOLS 68

CHAPTER 10: HOW TO MARKET YOURSELF CONFIDENTLY 72

CHAPTER 11: GETTING TO KNOW YOU 78

CHAPTER 12: OPTIMIZING YOUR RESUME AND COVER LETTER TO STAND OUT 92

CHAPTER 13: WHAT YOUR BODY SAYS ABOUT YOU 99

CHAPTER 14: PERSON JOB SEARCHES AS POTENTIAL INTERVIEWS 117

- CHAPTER 15: BEFORE THE INTERVIEW 125
- CHAPTER 16: INTERVIEW DO'S AND DON'TS 135
- CHAPTER 17: UNDERSTANDING THE SALARY OR HOURLY PAY 142
- CHAPTER 18: PRE-INTERVIEW ESSENTIALS 145
- CHAPTER 19: PRESENTATION AND GROOMING 151
- CHAPTER 20: SAMPLE INTERVIEW QUESTIONS AND ANSWERS 158
- CHAPTER 21: PRACTIC MAKES PERFECT 176
- CONCLUSION 191

Introduction

Do you want the keys on how to excel and land the job of your dreams? Are you new to the job market? A recent graduate? Changing careers? Or returning to the workforce? Well, read on! This guide is meant to help you get the job you deserve. Since research shows that most readers give up on a book in the early chapters, we decided to make this guide short and to the point so that you can extract the main elements you need to know in an hour or less.[1]

This guide has every aspect from resume preparation to interview etiquette to Human Resources follow-up covered in a detailed manner. All you need is a pen and paper to jot down some notes and you are ready to go. **Let's get started!**

Combined, Paul and Shannon have over 25 years of experience in the business world. Paul alone has over 10 years industry expertise in working as a residential leasing manager and licensed real estate agent. He has worked closely with tenants, attorneys, real estate agents, mortgage lenders and title insurance companies to help clients buy or rent homes. In addition, he has retail management experience at a large pharmaceutical company, as well as a business marketing role at a publishing firm. Paul has been introduced to situations that have helped shape his professional work portfolio and groom him to provide professional advice based on real-life work experience. He speaks to you through the pages of this guidebook using real-life application and experience to teach you how to handle the interview process from answering interview questions, proper etiquette, professional resume and cover letter presentation and research techniques.

Having been a finance and banking professional since 1998, Shannon addresses her audience through the eyes of a seasoned career woman, who has mastered many interviews, received several promotions and dealt with many Human Resources situations in her years in the workforce. Shannon has worked her way up in banking to a commercial lending role as a business loan administrator, commercial credit analyst, and a licensed residential mortgage loan officer.

We want you to get the most from this book so read it intently and more than once, if needed. Please be patient, consistent and try, try, try again! If you happen to get passed up the first or second time, chances are in your favor that your time is coming fast! Good things in life take time and your perfect career is no different.

First things first. You need to do a quick visual exercise based on your career goals.

In order to know exactly what direction this path will ultimately lead you on, you must first take a minute to jot down or think about two important elements so we can help you end up where you want to be with regards to your career path. These quick tasks are:

Planning and focusing on your objectives/goals – What careers has your education and/or work background prepared you for? Do you need additional schooling or classes to prepare for another career which you are more interested in? Remember, it is OK to change career paths if, once you have begun down a certain career path, it is not as fulfilling as you believed it to be at first.

Understanding the best job landing tools available – There are some excellent career search engines we have found to be very useful. They are as follows:

Indeed.com
Glassdoor.com
Monster.com
Careerbuilder.com
SimplyHired.com
LinkedIn job search network
ZipRecruiter.com

While there are many other excellent search engines, these are our favorite job-finding websites. You may find others that you like, so add them to your proverbial 'list' of search engines that you are likely to use.

Chapter 1: What Are The Types Of Job Interviews?

Job interviews have come a long way. It is not just the generic sitting in the same room and talking to the hiring officer. This day and age, with the diversity of jobs available, the types of interviews (and interviewers) have also become more varied. Here are a few of the most common ones:

1. One-On-One

Most typical of all, a one-on-one interview is the common first step after human resources has sifted through the pile of resumes and picked out the qualified ones. For massive companies, this first interview also determines if you will be shortlisted to go on another one-on-one interview with a manager, a supervisor or move to a panel interview.

2. Panel Interview

A panel interview is usually a higher level of interview—for those who have gone through one or two initial interviews. It is usually done for jobs that entail an entire team to work on a project, for higher position jobs or for international organizations. Panel interviews can be nerve-racking for many because it has at least three people of different positions and specializations. The goal of a panel interview is to ascertain if the applicant is really a good fit given the expectations and demands of different departments or teams.

3. Online Interview

Online interviews are those done over Skype or other VoIP providers. It is usually done for online employment or whenever the interviewer and applicant are from different parts of the world. Although some may say that online interviews tend to be less formal because of the lack of actual physical presence, it still should not be taken lightly. Online interviews still has the face-to-face aspect and still entails preparation, even though you may be wearing you comfy pajama bottoms unknown to the interviewer.

4. Phone Interview

Interviews over the phone have been around for a long time. This is mostly done for long distance communications, when the hiring party has less time to have face-to-face interactions. In most scenarios, phone interviews are follow-up interviews, after an initial one-on-one has already been done.

5. Interview Over Meals or Coffee

For some companies that are more relaxed or for jobs that are more person-specific, interviews are done over meals or coffee. This seemingly informal setting does not mean letting your guard down, as most employers who do this have a knack for getting to know applicants' personalities without the smoke and mirrors that is stiffness and predictability. Needless to say, interviews over meals or coffee can be tricky to navigate, especially if you are more used to the structured type of job interviews.

Knowing what kind of interview, you are scheduled for helps in the specifics of some prep work. Although there are general things to remember when preparing for any kind of interview.

Chapter 2: How To Pass Your Job Interview

The project analyze, that how a person can fare very well in an interview. It is purely enlighten a person to get through a job interview. Interviews are held for various job positions and the gravity of interview varies with the job position advertised. Globally methods of interviews are different from country to country and with multi national cultures. Whatever the fundamentals we observe it's almost every nation act on basic principles at interviews.

1. Why interviews are important in selecting / recruiting a person for a job?

Every company / organization has their own culture, vision & mission and targets to achieve. Today in the global industry arena, there is a tough competition in developing / promoting the businesses. They have to appoint best persons with academic qualifications and professional skills to face challenges and reach their targets. Therefore always they prefer to select persons who are capable to drive over the business challenges.

2. What is interview competency?

Interview competency is a very important factor. This equally applies to interviewers and interviewees. In organizations, interview boards should consist with knowledgeable and competent bodies. Particularly interview board should have excellent knowledge, criteria, country's employment law, employment conditions and salary terms of the job position. Competency standards of interviews, therefore plays a prominent role when selecting the most suitable person to job position. Similarly person facing interview also should have at least fair knowledge of interview competency. It's of immense importance that interviewee should gather above information and study about before in advance the interview. Then he / she will be strong to answer any questions of interview board to the exact point

3. What's job interview? What it covers?

Job interviews can be categorized as Preliminary Interview, First Interview and Final Interview. Job interviews will come up due to vacancies occur or when organizations create new job positions, probably with company expansions. Main objective of an interview is to select most suitable, qualified skilled persons for job positions.

4. Preliminary Interview

HR Department will screen and short list candidates after a thorough process with the assistance of the Manager or Head of Department, where vacancy exists. Only a selected number of candidates who commensurate with required qualifications and experience will be called for this interview. According to company's requirement preliminary interview can be conducted over the phone, Skype or follow up by emails because the time is very precious where everybody is concern. This is a process of out lining best candidates. Candidates should listen very well and answer to questions. In case of

Skype interview it's advisable to use a headset.

5. First Interview

Only selected candidates of preliminary interview will be called for a personal interview. Interview board will go through your academic/professional qualifications, inspect all certificates, work samples and any other printed matter. Candidates are supposed to be well prepared with their certificates to prove competencies. They will definitely question you about your past experience and employment history. There should not be any gaps (periods of unemployment) in your employment history because it may lead to unnecessary suspicions. If there are any such gaps you must be able to produce valid and acceptable reasons.

Practical Skill Test

In some organizations they give certain practical skill test

Example: If the job position for an Engineering Assistant, interview board detail them with a skill test to draw an engineering drawing or to assemble some unit of a machine. (This test varies with different job positions) In my point of view this is a very effective test because you can never judge a candidate's skills merely by paper qualifications. Definitely candidates with advanced skills, score best marks at this test. Therefore it's of immense important that you have to be thorough with your practical work too.

6. Final Interview

Very best candidates selected over merits of first interview will be interviewed finally. Probably three or four candidates will get qualified for final interview. At this stage HR Manager will check their references and other valid factors, in advance of the interview. Usually salary terms, availability, medical test and some other very important factors will be discussed and checked with candidates. Considering marks scored in first interview, practical test and final interview now it's very easy to make the final selection, provided if the interviews are conducted in a professional manner.

Standard Specimen Marking Scheme is given below (liable to change as per various company requirements)

Presentation for interview: 15
Academic Qualifications: 20
Professional Qualifications: 20
Experience: 20
Drive / job knowledge / skills: 25
Total marks: 100

With my vast exposure to HR management, I have experienced that candidates very seldom get above 70 marks. It's suitable to consider candidates score maximum marks over 65.

Companies can design their own marking schemes, depending on their employment categories and other governing factors. We have reaped better results by adopting above formula.

PREPARING FOR THE INTERVIEW

1. Pre study about the organization

It's wise to do a pre study about the organization where the vacancy exists. Interview Board always sees how much you are interested on the job. If the job is very fitting to you gather information about the place and be prepared. There are many sources that will help you to gather information. You may do a web research, read magazines, bulletins or any other printed media. Following factors will be important to you.

• Company Establishment, year established.
• Registration details of company
• Nature of Business
• Lay out of company – Headquarters, sub offices, branches
• Name of the Chairman / CEO
• Board of Directors if any
• Key positions of the company & position holders
• Employment strength

If you can gather at least such basic information you are now little stronger than you were. Interview panel sometimes raises a question, why do you want to join this company? Now you have some stuff to answer. They will be shocked by your answer and might put more questions to you; such as what else do you know about us? When you give a prompt answer they will definitely have some interest on you. Anybody can do well if you are interested on it, if you have no interest on the work you perform, it will end up a failure. A person who likes ice cream would not be satisfied with a plantain. It's a simple and absolute truth. Always company managements will observe people interested in work.

2. Your personality Development

In advance of the interview you have to develop your personality. When interviewing people I have observed that they comply with all job requirements but seem to be very backward, frightened and shy to face the interview. Most of the bright candidates lack in personality and they loose nice job opportunities. Think positive, work positive and answer positive. To achieve this standard it's compulsory to build & develop your personality.

3. Notifying your referees about the interview

Never attend interviews without prior informing to your referees, whom you have named as referees in your application. Interviewers might refer to them without your knowledge; it makes your referees uncomfortable. If you have informed them in advance about the interview, they will expect some body referring to him. As well keep your Employer / immediate superiors informed in advance. Always pick some genuine people to recommend you.

4. Dress code for interview

Please select a suitable dress code that gives you a smart & professional look. Ladies can be dressed with normal office uniform; can wear slack & coat or a sari to match the occasion. You can carry your brief case, hand bag or document holder. Please try to avoid unnecessary make ups because it's only an interview; not a function or dress parade. Determine to be smart and pleasant looking.

5. Final check up before setting off for interview

Have you replied to your interview letter, thanking them for considering for the interview?

If so take with you the interview letter you received along with your national identity, certificates, work samples and Letters of Appointments of past employments etc.

6. Punctuality

Reach the interview venue in time, (little in advance to scheduled time) Give them an impression that you are punctual. Reaching well before time is not advisable; you must show that you have no time just to spend without an engagement. This is really a time management factor.

7. Waiting till you are called

You have to wait patiently till you are called for the interview. Keep up to your manners, do not converse with the staff of that company or do not try to gather any information from them. When you reach there, produce your interview letter to the reception and politely answer to any questions of the receptionist. When your turn comes you will be accompanied by some member of the organization up to the entrance of the interview room. If the door is closed gently tap the door and enter the room, leave the door at the former position where it was when you enter without making any noise. Determine that interview Board will observe all your movements. You should know that interview board will apply some interview techniques on you on and off. You must be able to identify them and act accordingly.

In the same manner you can apply your interview techniques on interview board when it's required. At any stage you should not enter the interview arena with an exited face. You have to be quite normal and in a leisure mood. Once after entering interview room you may wish the interview board, when the seat is offered you can sit. Now you can shake hands with the members of interview panel, then you may briefly introduce yourself to them. Answer their questions in a pleasing mood. If four persons are there in the interview panel, sometimes they put questions to you one after the other. Now this chapter is very important. By putting questions from all the corners they see whether you are getting exited. Interviewee has to be a very good listener. What you should do is answer to the first person who asks you the question. Also always keep eye contacts with the person to whom you are answering. (It has some sort of physiological effect) one of the interview techniques commonly used by interviewers. In my experience, I have noticed that candidates loose eye contacts when they lie to interview board. They will not continue that toughness once they understand that you are genuine. So now you know the first stage of the interview is bit tough. When first impression is good, you get the green light on to continue rest of the interview with determination and courage.

Now they will start to check your qualifications, work samples etc. Your answers to the questions should very well match with what you have stated in your resume. Checking on employment history, there should not be gaps between employment periods. Such information may lead to unnecessary suspicions.

Probably they may subject you to a practical skill test to examine your practical job knowledge. In an early paragraph I have explained that how much of value can be added to a candidate by a practical test. So you have to be thorough with your practical work if you are serious to secure the job. Do not forget that interview is a competition among candidates. The person who performs up to the expectations, deliver work of best quality and with best time duration will get highest score. Any organization is looking for best workers to promote their missions.

Chapter 3: Preparing To Answer Anticipated Job Interview Questions

Some common questions usually make an appearance at most job interviews. To ace that important job interview, prepare for these questions as well as other questions an interviewer is likely to ask you. Use the information you gathered earlier about the company and your interviewers to come up with other anticipated questions. To get you started on this process, below are questions usually asked at job interviews along with their right replies.

1: Please Tell Us about Yourself

Most interviewers will most likely ask you to give a short description of yourself. When asked this question, the interviewers are giving you a chance to give a detailed account of your life so far—especially in relation to how the experiences in your life have equipped you for the job at hand. This question asks that you to give a little introduction into who you are, what you have done so far, your education, and your employment history.

You can also talk a little about your interests and passions. Keep this answer under a minute long because lengthy descriptions may bore the interviewers.

2: What Have You Gathered So Far About Our Company?

An interviewer (or several of them) will ask you this question as phrased above or as **"What do you know or have learned about this company?"** Both questions require you to give the interviewers basic information about the company, its history, its achievements, its position in the industry, and the products/services it deals in. This is where all the homework/research you conducted on the company will come in handy and will help you state a compelling answer.

3: Why Are You Interested In This Job?

This question seeks to help interviewers understand your attraction towards the job you are interviewing for and why you are thinking of leaving your current job if you are in any form of employment. To answer this question effectively, clarify the designation you're applying for as well as the job description so you know what you will be doing for that business or company or where your interest in the job comes from.

For instance, if you're applying for the position of a senior content writer and editor of a magazine, you know you will most likely have to manage writers under you and ensure the final content is written well, is devoid of all sorts of errors, and meets all the required standards. Therefore, while talking about your interest in that position, you can tell the interviewers that you're looking forward to managing people and showcasing your talents as a writer, which is why this job appeals to you.

4: Why Do You Want to Leave Your Current Job?

The interviewers would want to know why you're so keen on leaving your current job for the one you're interviewing for. First, interviewers want to make sure you did not lose your last job because of any illegal activity or any reason that makes you unfit for the job you're applying for. This helps them ensure they hire people who have a clean working history; people who're not criminally inclined.

Secondly, they want to make sure you are not in the habit of jumping from one job to the next. No sane business or company wants to hire someone who switches jobs every few months. Companies are looking for sincere, dedicated employees who are committed to improving and growing the business or company. If you are in the habit of switching jobs, the employer is likely to deem you unfit for the job you are applying for.

Thirdly, this answer also helps the interviewer/s determine your interest in the job and company/business. For instance, if you are leaving your current job because it did not have any scope for growth but the post in the company you are interviewing for provides you with many growth opportunities, they know you will be more enthusiastic in their job and are likely to stay long-term.

5: What are Your Greatest Strengths and Weaknesses?

The interviewers want to know your biggest assets and weaknesses so they know what you will be offering them and how you can benefit their company or business. Your weaknesses give them a glimpse of your shortcomings.

While outlining your strengths, state and describe any 3 to 5 of your biggest strengths. Often, the interviewers will ask you to enumerate 3 or a maximum of 5 strengths; if they don't define a number, do not go on and on about how amazing you are. Stick to the point and list 5 of your biggest strengths. This should include any of your skills, qualities, or potentials you are proud of and preferably, those that highlight your idealness for the job at hand or how you will benefit their company.

For instance, if your strengths include being a good team leader, have excellent design skills, work well under pressure, good analytical and writing skills, and good cooking skills, if you're applying for the post of a web analyst who needs to manage a team of 5 designers, you need not highlight the last strength because cooking is not a prerequisite for the job.

When asked about your weaknesses, please do not state "I don't have any weakness," or say you are a perfectionist when you're not. These answers are clichés and often not true. While the interviewers are looking for great candidates that work well under pressure and can do their work to the best of their abilities, they are not looking for superheroes and if you tell them you're perfect, they won't buy that hogwash and are likely not to consider for you the position.

Hence, when answering this question, be honest and state any three of your weaknesses that you wish to improve on. Briefly describe how that weakness limits you and assure the interviewer that you are working on your weaknesses so that you can improve.

6: Please Describe Your Work Style/Method

Most interviewers will ask you to highlight your work style so they can understand how you will work on different aspects of your job i.e. if you get the job or the projects you'll have to undertake. Are you in the habit of waiting for the last minute to complete important projects or do you move in a smooth, organized manner?

The interviewers are most likely looking for people who manage their time effectively and efficiently, individuals who complete their projects before a deadline so they can have time to review it and thus minimize errors.

If that's not your working style, be honest about it. Honesty goes a long way; if your work style has previously helped you stay productive and manage your work successfully, describe it in detail so you can help the interviewers understand how that style helps you.

7: How Do You Think You'll Benefit Our Company or Why Do You Think You're a Good Fit for this Job?

Interviewers want to know what makes you good enough or an appropriate fit for this job; they want to know how you expect to become an asset for their company. They obviously don't want to waste time on people who cannot bring anything special to the table. This is where you need to highlight your special skills and strengths and use the information you gathered about the company and their competitors so you can create a compelling answer to convince them of your unique qualification for the job at hand.

For instance, if you're good at research and development, a skill you used to help the previous company you were working for reduce their product manufacturing costs by 15%, and you know one of the strengths of the competitors of this company is that they offer affordable products, you can tell your interviewers that you can easily help their company reduce their manufacturing costs without compromising the quality of the product. Describe how you expect to achieve this.

8: Where Do You See Yourself in 5 to 10 Years?

Interviewers want to know your plans for the future so they know whether you intend to provide value to their company for a long or short time. Whatever your plans are for the next 5 to 10 years, describe them honestly irrespective of whether or not you wish to work in this company for that long. However, if you're not sure about what you will want after a year or two, let them know you are a committed person and plan to grow better in this company. If one of your interviewers is your boss and you wish to take over his position in the future, don't clearly state your motives because your answer may turn him into your opponent. Just let them know you seek growth.

9: What Salary Do You Expect from Us?

Interviewers often ask about your salary requirements; state them clearly keeping in mind the working hours and your job requirements. Also, use your previous salary as a basis to demand more or less from this job depending on its requirements.

10: Do You Have Any Questions or Want to Ask Anything We Did not cover?

Interviewers will often give you an opportunity to clear your ambiguities in the end or ask any questions you have. Now is a good time to ask the following questions:

What are the available growth opportunities in this company? This question helps you know the scope of growth in the company, which will be important for you if wish to grow bigger and better with time.

What sort of bonuses and incentives do you offer your employees?

Will I be responsible only for the work highlighted in the description or will I have to complete extra work that does not fall under the category?

Will there be times when I have to work late?

What guidance will I receive in case of challenging projects?

Whom do I need to report to and who will be reporting to me?

When and how frequently do you conduct your performance appraisals?

Do you offer your employees medical or other services and benefits?

If there are any other questions you wish to ask, list them down on a piece of paper (prior to the interview) and go through them a few times so you don't forget any important point. You can also take that paper with you on the interview day.

Go through these questions a few times and use them to prepare effective and compelling answers. The key to impressing your interviewers is to answer confidently. The next section tells you how to do that.

Chapter 4: Take Care Of Your Resume

Your resume represents you. It is the only solid proof of all that you are capable of after having graduated from a reputed university. The role that a resume plays in your prospects of landing a good job cannot be put in words. It is your face when it comes to representing you to the interviewers. Do not ignore your resume. Take care of it in three simple steps.

Step I: Building of a Resume

The process of building your resume should ideally start as soon as you leave school and enter a good college. Right from that random debate competition you won to any relay race you participated in- everything is to be recorded with all the due information filled in, in your resume.

It is necessary that you start off really early. A resume contains all your achievements and participations. It does not matter what natured competitions you took part in. A resume isn't particular in nature; it shows you grown in overall.

Hence, you need to mention everything you have attained so far.

Maintain an internship diary. When you intern, you build goodwill and trust with companies and groups of people you intern with or under. Make sure everything goes in your internship diary and eventually makes its way into your resume.

Do not let go vacations waste. While they are meant to be for the purposes of fun and frolic, do not forget to devote one part of your vacations to keep looking for places to intern at. Enjoy your vacations but always keep in mind the possible places you can work at for what better time than vacations to build your resume.

The first stage of your resume building is filling quality content in it. This can be achieved by participating in competitions and presentations. It does not matter if you win competitions or not. At times, mere participations score you brownie points.

Step II: Technicalities of Resume

An ideal resume contains all your details in a structured format. Usually, a resume has the following details regarding you:

● Your full name.

● Your permanent address. Generally, this address is the place you were born in or your ancestral place where your ancestors still reside.

● Your current address. The point of including current address is to allow chances of easy access to you in case phone numbers and emails do not work.

● Phone number (s), along with STD and state code numbers. If you are selected, they will require to contact. A phone call is the easiest way to do so. Keep in mind that the number you frequently use should be provided.

● Detailed information regarding your achievements. Often, corporate offices want to verify your claims so it is honorable to provide them all the necessary knowledge regarding the competitions you took part in.

● Your interest list is another space that needs to be cleverly filled. This space is usually at the end of a resume so as to convey casualness to the applicant. But very few realize the importance of this space. Say, you are applying for a job at a prestigious law firm. If you mention that you are interested in family laws, they will be inclined towards allotting you a place in their family law department.

● Another very casual looking space that a resume requires you to fill is one named 'Passions in life'. People usually mention their hobbies. Best candidates are reading, music, poetry and athletics. This part of a resume lets the employers know about your overall personality. Do not leave his space blank as it would show that besides academics you have no life.

Step III: Fine tuning your resume

Before pressing the 'send' button on the email containing your resume, go over your resume looking for any-

A. Flaws with regards to your filling up

B. Filling up technical slip ups

C. Wrong or misleading claims

Think twice before writing anything in your resume. It may so happen that what you are writing down isn't even required. Fill up the most important parts first and then move further to the less significant ones. If possible, forward the resume to someone close for proof-reading.

The last stage of making a good resume is all about making sure there is nothing lacking or misleading in it. You can choose to go through your resume more than five times and yet find nothing wrong with it. It's always wiser to forward it to a third party who is at a better position to point out flaws in your resume.

A good resume is the most important part of your hunting journey. Ignoring this will lead to rejection and regret. A well maintained and structured resume can work wonders even if you have fewer qualifications than someone more deserving.

Chapter 5: Networking And Building Professional Relationships

It is important for every career person to build alliances. Although knowledge and skills are important to be successful, a person also needs to maintain a strong professional network. Although a lot of people may be intimidated by networking, it is important to realize that there are different ways to build professional relationships. If you're not comfortable to network in large groups, you can start by one-on-one networking. You don't have to worry about what you have to say. You just have to make it a point to ask other people about their work and themselves. Networking lets you know other professionals. It also lets other people get to know you.

What Can Your Network Do

Your network can offer solutions to your difficult problem. These people can offer perspective and can even teach you a lot of things. They can provide information about new opportunities and can be supportive of your efforts. They celebrate with you when you succeed and offer valuable feedback when needed. They can be your stress-relievers and introduce you to other people as well.

Who Can Be in Your Network

Your network can include people who can help you in various ways. They can be people adept with technology, peers, social contacts, people with external perspectives, people with organizational awareness, people with business knowledge, people with different backgrounds, and people who are knowledgeable about your customers.

You can also build your network in various ways. You can attend events and meetings to meet new people. You can join an online network. You can invite your colleagues to coffee, lunch, or other gatherings to get to know them better. You can work on cross-departmental or cross-functional teams. You can also attend training programs and classes or volunteer on projects where you can use your expertise.

How To Build Your Network

You can't build your network if you don't want to share information and resources with other people because networking is a symbiotic relationship. You have to give so that you can also take. You have to learn to offer your expertise, skills, feedback, perspective, and insights. You have to search for opportunities for you to make contributions and offers. In addition, you have to maintain contact with your network members. You have to learn to ask other people for referrals to other people who may be of help to you or whom you can help.

The Power Of Social Networking

Social networking combines the power of the Internet and traditional networking. It provides an opportunity for people to form a community of virtual contracts. There are also a lot of community forums and discussions groups which you can join online. If you don't feel comfortable about face-to-face interactions, you'll surely enjoy these virtual groups. In addition, you expand your contacts exponentially and receive immediate responses. You have access to a lot of people through the Internet.

If you're going to network online, please ensure that you use your real name and not an alias. You have to follow basic business etiquette and ensure that you understand the privacy settings of the social media you're using.

Building Successful Professional Relationships

A lot of people are uncomfortable about networking because they feel that it's just a way of exchanging business cards and shaking hands. They fail to notice that these are what everyone does every day. Basically, networking is building and maintaining relationships.

For a lot of people who know the importance of networking, they still prefer face-to-face interactions because they find it easy to build understanding and trust if they meet in person. It is advisable to meet about 5 contacts for lunch or coffee each week. However, it's not enough just to pay lip-service to build connections. You have to be prepared to help those who needed assistance while you seek help for yourself. You should feel honored if people ask you for guidance and help because relationships are built this way.

Networking is a very important platform to share insights, experience, and knowledge. Relationships are important if you want to grow your professional career. Networking doesn't only secure business opportunities but it also inspires collaboration, and sharing of information and ideas.

Some Interview Questions And Answers

Question: How would your boss and coworkers describe you?

Why this may be asked: The interviewer wants to know about your relationships and your role in your team. This question will give the interviewer an idea of how fit you are with the job duties within a team structure. It focuses on your human qualities and personality.

Possible answer: If the interviewer is a manager, he wants to know if you're the answer to his myriads of problems. He wants to know how you work with a team and how you handle conflicts. He also wants to know how you can improve a team's effectiveness and efficiency. He wants to know if you can fit in his team. In case, there are some future coworkers interviewing you, they want to know about your work ethic and attitude. They want to size you up if you can get along well with them.

If there are future coworkers who are interviewing you, you have to include qualities like trustworthy, dependable, sense of humor, hardworking, considerate, easygoing, and positive. You can say, "I am willing to help my coworkers when needed. I also offer help without being asked."

"I like building strong relationships with my team because I'll be spending a lot of hours daily with them for a long time."

"I like having fun when it's appropriate. I know how to keep tension low and morale high."

If only the manager is interviewing you, you can include qualities like efficient, dependable, great energy, hardworking, dedicated, positive, organized, reliable, and punctual. You can say, "I am a team player and I offer help to my coworkers to get the job done."

"I am a situational leader when a non-critical decision has to be made or when there's conflict."

"I like to build up team morale and have fun because if there's a positive atmosphere, everyone becomes more productive."

Instead of using your imagination about what your coworkers would say, you can include some testimonials in your answer. You can say, "My former coworker at XXX Company, John Doe, said that I can make even the most grouchy customer smile."

"My co-employee nominated for "Employee of the Month" award because I tried to make his work easier."

"My coworker Alice said that I'm professional and organized. She even volunteered to write a recommendation letter for me."

Testimonials offer authority and extra weight because this means that you're not making your answers up. You use your real coworkers in your reply. You can ask your coworkers to make testimonials for you before you go for an interview so that you can include them in your application.

Question: How do you handle a difficult coworker?

Why this may be asked: The interviewer wants to know how you'll react if there's interpersonal conflict. He wants to know if you have a firm grasp of your reactions. He wants to have an idea of your relationship-building skills.

Possible answer: You want your interviewer to know that you don't agitate your coworkers nor hide or run away from them. You have to be professional in dealing with them so that your relationships with them will be more positive.

"I'm not easily drawn into conflicts with colleagues. If it's not avoidable, I will state my opinion in a polite manner. Even if there are conflicting points of view, communication is still important. I don't believe in aggressiveness but I don't also run away from confrontations. I try to understand my coworkers because it's the more productive way to handle the situation. I try to seek a common ground and find a way to iron out any difficulties."

Question: What is an ideal team for you?

Why this may be asked: The interview wants to find out how you perceive a successful team to be. He wants to gain useful information about your compatibility and capabilities. He wants to know if you're a team player.

Possible answer: Teamwork requires effective communication; understanding and recognizing other people's viewpoints; appreciation of the contributions you can make; and the building interpersonal relationships. You have to let the interviewer know that you have a clear understanding of what teamwork means.

"A successful team is composed of people who value communication. By working with fellow team members, I have to communicate with them, and understand, recognize, and appreciate them. I have to ensure that we trust each other to ensure that our team will be successful. Respect is also important if we're to work well together."

Chapter 6: Taking Inventory Of Your Qualifications

By now, you have identified your jobs of interest and compiled a list of the qualifications associated with those jobs. It is now time to conduct an inventory of your skills and qualifications so that you can measure them against your job or career-specific qualifications. This is an important step in that you **must** have an understanding of how your qualifications stack up against those associated with your jobs of interest if you are to develop an effectiveplan of attack. For example, if the job requires a Bachelor's degree and you only possess an Associate's, then you know you have some work to do. It is important to evaluate not only the **hard skills** such as education, technical proficiency, or language skills, but also the **soft skills**, those associated with interpersonal relationships (e.g. communication skills, time management, or work ethic, to name a few). The key to assessing your qualifications is to think about the **value** you can add to a particular organization. Remember, you are selling yourself as a solution to a company's problem. For example, if the job calls for **critical thinking** skills, you may question whether you possess that trait; however, think about all of the times you solved a particular problem or contributed toward the solution of a problem. What skills did you use? Do not sell yourself short. Chances are that you have what it takes to do the job; you just need to articulate it.

An easy way to assess your qualifications is to list specific job criterion for each job of interest and then give serious thought about how you measure up. It is also advantageous to identify prospective interviewees within the companies in which your jobs of interest are located. The reason for this is that when you conduct your informational interview, you will be able to reference the jobs you applied to within the interviewee's firm, and then be able to speak specifically to the criteria associated with a particular job. In doing so, it signals to the interviewee that you have done your homework. Even better, if things go well, the interviewee may be able to help you secure one of the jobs for which you have applied. Even if you are familiar with a particular industry, the more intelligently you can speak to the qualifications of a **specific position**within the interviewee's organization, the better he or she will judge you. The more information you are armed with and the better prepared you are, the more an interviewee is likely to view you as a potential asset to their organization.

As you identify your jobs, you compare and contrast your qualifications with those of the position to identify the gaps. The gaps you identify are the challenges you must overcome, which also become the basis for many of questions you ask the interviewee during the informational interview. What I mean here is that when you identify gaps in qualifications, your job will be to seekthe interviewee's opinion on how to best to overcome those gaps.

Measuring your qualifications against those commonly found in your area of interest can be a time consuming process. However, the time you spend doing the grunt work will pay dividends in terms of helping you articulate a clear understanding of what your limitations may be. Once you have taken inventory of your qualifications, you will have a much better picture of where you stand. More importantly, you will have a solid understanding of the value you can add.

If you remember nothing else, remember this: The brand you are selling is YOU. Your product (i.e., qualifications) are the

solutions you can offer. This is a concept you will want to keep in the forefront of your mind whenever interacting with people who have the potential to open doors or hire you.

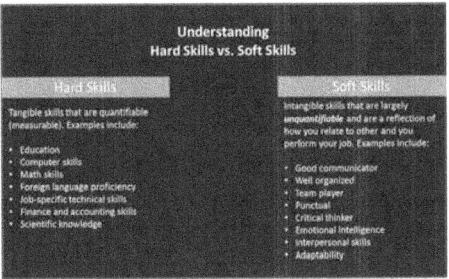

Increasingly, employers are basing hiring decisions on how finely developed an applicant's soft skills might be. Employers are looking for people who exemplify the organization's values, who can represent the company with distinction, and who can work well with others. The need to possess soft skills cannot be overstated. There is a saying that goes: Hard skills might get you the interview, but Soft skills get you the job.

Chapter 7: Building A Confident Resume

Search engines are key to getting a job in today's job market. Every minute of every day, recruiters and employers are entering keywords into search engines to find job candidates. To get your next job, you need to play the keyword game.

In this chapter, I'll discuss ways to find what keywords an employer will look for on your resume and how to weave those words into your resume's content.

We commonly type keywords into search engines such as Google or Yahoo! in hopes of pulling up information we seek. In much the same way, a recruiter trying to fill a job enters keywords into a search engine online or in a resume database to find ideal candidates' resumes.

Keywords are terms (one word or a few strung together) that capture the essence of a topic. When looking for a job online, use as many keywords in your search as necessary (such as job title, skills, zip code) to pull up job posts that match your qualifications.

This explains why it's so important for your resume to contain all the keywords for the job you're going for. You want your resume to pop up in the recruiter's search results window—and you want your resume to be at or near the top of that list of results. How will you manage that? By making sure your resume has every single keyword and its acronym (for example, "Project Management Office" and "PMO") that a recruiter might possibly key into the search engine.

Here's how you can make that happen:

1. Create a list of keywords for the job you seek.

2. Incorporate them into your resume.

Sounds easy enough, doesn't it? With a computer at your fingertips, it's a quick process.

The Job Title

Before you sit down to write your resume, you need to figure out what job you're going for. Why? Because that job title (your job objective) is one of the most important keywords on your resume.

Think of your resume as a marketing piece that you'll post on the Internet. Like any good online marketing piece, it should be filled with all the terms a recruiter's search engine uses to find someone like you. You may ask, "Can't I make a generic resume, and then decide what job I want?" I highly recommend you not use a generic resume. Instead, take the following steps:

1. Research job possibilities in the industry and occupation you've chosen.

2. Find job postings for specific jobs in that line of work that you can and want to do.

3. Print out (or save to your computer) job posts that you want to respond to.

4. If you find more than one job (and you likely will), prioritize those posts so your first choice is on top.

5. Create a targeted resume for job choice number one that includes all the keywords from that job post.

6. Make a copy of your resume for job choice number one, and adjust it so it's targeted for job choice number two.

7. For each job post that you respond to, tailor your resume for that specific job, paying attention to appropriate keywords for each post.

A targeted resume is created for a very specific job or line of work. It contains keywords and qualifications that unmistakably define its job objective. Don't be lazy about customizing your resume. Your investment of time and energy to make a targeted resume for each application will pay off.

Drumming Up the Right Keywords

An easy way to use the right keywords for a particular job is to ...

1. Print out the job post.

2. Highlight or underline the keywords in the job post.

3. Write statements or create lists that contain those keywords on your resume.

Trolling for Your Ideal Job

What if you're not applying for a specific job, but rather simply putting your resume up on one of the huge job boards for a recruiter to find? How can you tailor that resume? Easy! Write a resume for your ideal job. Here's how:

1. Write a job description for your ideal job, using your imagination to picture exactly what the job would entail and what sort of company culture you want that job to be in (for example, young and hip, or traditional and conservative).

2. Make a list of keywords that define all the things you want in that job (for instance, working with "teens" or doing "outside sales").

3. Write your resume for the ideal job you've just described, being sure to include all the keywords from your list. If you follow these steps, your marketing piece has a strong chance of drawing your ideal job to you. Wouldn't that be cool?

Chapter 8: How To Excel In An Interview

Speaking the Best Body Language

As you continue to prepare for a job interview, you should not forget about your body language. Do you cross your hands whenever you are nervous or play with your hair while thinking of an answer? Well, you need to avoid them because they might distract the interviewer. Most of us have things we do when we are in a high-stress situation. Experts have been able to analyze certain body movements as a way to ascertain the character of a person. So, when going for an interview, consider the following body language tips.

Sit back in your seat - The first thing you should do is to sit firmly and lean your back straight against your chair. It is an automatic signal of confidence and assurance.

Make direct face contact - Rather than make direct eye contact, you can make a face contact. Allowing your gaze to be on other parts of the face of the hiring manager at frequent intervals is an effective way to appear interested and engaged. Rotate your eyes and lips, so you do not end up looking directly into the hiring manager's eyes.

Make use of hand gestures - Are you unsure of what to do with your hand? Well, you can gesture with them while speaking. Humans tend to conceal their hands when they are nervous because they tend to express our anxiety. However, when you keep your hands hidden, it could be misinterpreted as a distrustful behavior.

Open your palms - Opening your palms while speaking is a sign of engagement and honesty. In fact, experts say that the limbic brain picks up the positivity and this makes the hiring manager comfortable. This explains why we shake hands just to show open palms. Generally, upward-facing body languages like smiles, straight posture and open palms make you look energetic.

Place your feet on the ground- You should place your feet firmly on the ground. In addition, rather than cross at the knees, women should cross at the ankles, which will enable them to switch when necessary without being obvious. Scientifically, unless you keep both of your feet on the ground, it will be difficult for you to answer questions that are highly complex. According to experts, this is connected with your ability to easily go back and forth between the limbic reptilian brain to the neocortex brain. Therefore, when translated to a layman's term, "a planted feet can assist you to go between creative thought and thoughts that are highly complex and rational."

Focus on your walk - Most times, hiring managers make their judgment within 10 seconds of meeting with an applicant, so the way you walk into the room is also part of the decision they make. Endeavor to pull back your shoulders and make sure your neck is elongated. Make each of your strides roughly one to two feet wide and walk directly toward the interviewer with every part of your body pointing toward her direction. Maintain eye contact with occasional breaks to the side.

Learn to breathe deeply - You can soothe your nerves during an interview by breathing properly. When the interviewer asks you a question, inhale and speak on the exhale following the airflow. Deep breathing is known to calm us down when we are stressed. So, take ten deep diaphragmatic breaths before the interview so it can help reduce your heart rate, stress hormone level and blood pressure.

Nod your head appropriately - Apart from maintaining eye and face contact, you can show attentiveness by nodding your head while listening. You will give the hiring manager the impression that you are enjoying the session and understand what they said by nodding your head occasionally.

Know when to Lean in - When you are engaged in a conversation, leaning in is a natural thing to do. So, lean slightly forward and make sure you keep your shoulders back and down while keeping your chest high. This signifies interest.

Always remember that your posture remains an integral aspect of the nonverbal conversation. Therefore, you must consciously take advantage of them and increase your chances of success. In case you are being interviewed via a call, then consider walking while on the phone call. It will help you synchronize the left and right hemisphere of your brain, which will enhance your answers positively

Take Advantage of the "Tell me about yourself" Question

When attending an interview, certain questions are compulsory which you must answer regardless of your experience level, industry or type of job. The question that tops the list is "Tell me about yourself". Because it is the first question you are likely going to be asked, knowing the best thing to answer is an opportunity to make an outstanding first impression.

Expect this question from the interviewer as he attempts to get you talking. You will be asked this question possibly after a few chats about the weather or traffic.

Most applicants dread this question because they seem confused about what the hiring manager wants to know. However, when you prepare properly, then you do not have any reason to be scared. Rather, the question serves as an opportunity to emphasize the points you want your potential employer to know about you. Avoid wasting the opportunity by reciting your resume or hobbies and personal preferences. Your response needs to be concise and enthusiastic, and it should summarize how you are the best fit for the job. So, how can you answer the question?

Focus on the things you do that are related to the job. Reflect on three to five experiences you find relevant to the job you are applying for. Also, write down three to five of your strengths that are pertinent to the position such as skills, experiences, traits, and several others. This will increase the quality of the message you want the hiring manager to have about you.

The next thing you should do is to write out a script, which will include all the information you earlier listed. Start by talking about your past experiences as well as results and accomplishments. For instance:

"For the past six years, I have been in the customer service industry. My most recent role has been attending to incoming calls in the financial industry. One of the specific reasons why I enjoy this role as well as the challenges associated with it is the chance to connect with other people.

"I established remarkable customer relationships in my last job leading to a 30 percent increase in sales within seven months."

It is also important to mention some of your strengths so the next thing to write will be your strengths and abilities. Consider the example below:

"My strength is paying attention to detail. I have a strong reputation for following through and meeting set deadlines. Once I commit to do something, I ensure it's done on time."

You can conclude by talking about your current situation;

"I am looking for a company that truly values customer relations, a company with a strong team and a positive impact on sales and customer retention."

Practice

After writing down your answer based on the explanations, then practice until you feel confident about the things you want to emphasize in your response. You will remain focused by using the script, but do not make the mistake of memorizing it so you will not sound like a robot or someone reading the news. You have to sound as natural as possible. This information will help you in answering other questions too. While answering this question, avoid disclosing personal information such as your children, political or religious affiliations, marital status, etc. because they could work against you. Also, do not give multiple vague strengths without providing tangible examples to support them. This is also a conversation you must not rush, so you need to focus on answering the question accurately.

Chapter 9: Other Important Tools

REFERENCES

It has become commonplace to leave references off resumes with a statement at the bottom such as "references available upon request." Some clever job seekers think this is a great way to shorten their resumes. Remember earlier when we said always make things as easy as possible for an employer? Providing references makes things easier on employers. If you're making things difficult for them before you're even hired, chances are they won't be particularly interested in hiring you. Especially if they are 10 more resumes on the employers desk with references.

If you've tried your best and can't fit references on your one-page resume, you may include a separate references page. Just make sure that your contact information is listed on it as well, in the event that it gets separated from the rest of your information.

Social Media

Different careers require different must-haves. In this day and age of cyber connectivity, it's very likely a good idea to have a small website. Even if it just has your picture, resume, and a link or two to something career related that you're proud of, having a website shows you're willing to go the extra mile and do something to get noticed.

More importantly, if potential employers like what they see, they very likely will do an internet search of you either before or after an interview. Of course the best thing to do is never to put anything on social media that you don't want a potential employer to see. More than one politician's career has ended over old pictures and posts. But even if you never plan to run for office, or have any idea what the two main political parties in American government are called, be careful what you post. You never know when an interested employer might be turned off by shots of potential employees at a raging kegger or other inappropriate photos.

Make sure your social media pages are well protected from outside eyes and then double check those security features. Many social media sites are not as secure as you might assume. A prime example of this is Facebook. While users can choose their friends and take security measures for who can friend them and see their pages, people can still follow users without their permission. In addition, those who have the app on their phones, can be tracked as they travel to and from home, work, shop and dine. Facebook is not the only example of this. Plenty of social media sites have similar loopholes. These loopholes just may be the thing employers come across when conducting a background check on potential employees. Once hired, be mindful of posts as well. It's not uncommon to hear stories about employees who call in sick and then post pictures of themselves hanging out at the beach. Or maybe work has been tense, and insulting posts about a boss or another employee surface. Maybe, it happened at a past job. The bottom line? Nothing on the Internet goes away forever and eventually everyone gets access to it. Don't post anything you don't want the world to know. Employers are people too and they use the Internet.

Chapter 10: How To Market Yourself Confidently

All your hard work will finally pay off when your job hunt culminates in that much-coveted job interview — an opportunity to show employers what you have to offer. But keep in mind that how you present yourself on paper and in person are both absolutely crucial to the hiring process. Confidence is one of the biggest dealmakers in a job interview, but there is a big distinction between faking it and being authentically confident, and an even finer line between confident and arrogant.

The Line Between Confident and Cocky

The importance of projecting confidence during a job interview cannot be stressed enough; however, if you go overboard, you could rub potential employers the wrong way. Here are a few ways to stay in balance:

Be curious but not presumptuous. If you're asked questions about the department, or a particular type of project, share how you might approach it, but don't make any derogatory comments on the current management or situations.

Talk about yourself **by example only**. This means you don't need to say "I'm a good leader" or "I have initiative and I'm resourceful." Use examples and describe your achievements and career milestones. You can say, "I believe my leadership abilities will greatly benefit the company" and follow it up with an instance when your leadership skills shone. The best way to convey your strengths is to share examples that demonstrate them, much the same way in which a comedian doesn't tell you that he's funny, but tells you a joke instead and proves himself funny.

Master the art of the firm handshake. Practice with friends if you have to -- a good, firm handshake conveys confidence. A limp handshake communicates apprehension or weakness and a bone-crushing is not only painful, but may indicate insensitivity or over-assertiveness.

Speak at a moderate pace. Rapid speech can imply two things: It can make you appear anxious and nervous, or it can make you seem over-confident. Slow down and speak clearly and coherently. You can practice with friends for honest feedback and practice modulating your pace before the big day.

How to Maintain Poise

If you're asked a question you haven't prepared for, don't let the panic set in. Breathe deeply (but silently!), pause for a moment, and answer slowly. Or consider clarifying the question by restating it and confirming what the interviewer is looking for. This gives you a little time to process it, and the interviewer may even reframe the question in a way that gives you more insight into what they're looking for.

It's important to make eye contact for a couple of reasons. First, it helps establish rapport between you and the interviewer. And second, remember that the interviewer is only doing his or her job, looking out for the best interests of their organization. Remind yourself that whatever happens is OK – this is a person who, much like you, had to go through this same exact process.

How to Ditch the Jitters

Experiencing some anxiety before or during the interview is perfectly normal: even the most seasoned interviewees and applicants experience this. Here are some tips that should help calm your nerves and boost your confidence:

Work off excess energy. Exercise releases endorphins, which enhance a feeling of well-being. Consider doing a light workout well in advance of your interview if you can. Even if you can't get to the gym, doing some jumping jacks or running in place will help burn off some nervous energy. As a bonus, you can do some relaxing or stretching to get yourself in a calm state. Make sure to allow plenty of time to get clean, dressed, and go through your interview checklist.

Arrive early -- at least 15 minutes before the scheduled time -- to lessen the jitters and give you time to mentally prepare yourself. Use that time to take some deep breaths in the parking lot or while you're waiting in the lobby. Just inhale deeply from your nose, focusing on expanding your stomach or abdomen as you do so. As you exhale slowly (again through the nose), let your stomach relax and feel the rest of your body follow suit.

Visualize how the interview will go. As mentioned before, most fears come from the fear of the unknown, and job interviews can be quite unpredictable. Grab a pal a day before and do some role-playing to help you get in the mood. Ask your friend to be the interviewer so you can rehearse your answers beforehand.

Take note of your body movements. Avoid fidgeting, stretching, and grand gesticulations. Your body posture and movement should also be relaxed and confident.

If you feel that your hands are shaking, keep them still by clasping them together and placing them on your lap. Avoid crossing your arms — this body language might portray feeling fearful or defensive. Also avoid stretching as this can be interpreted as a sign of boredom. And avoid leaning too far back in your chair as it could be interpreted as being **overly** confident.

Give yourself a pep talk. You don't have to do this out loud, and you can do it up until you actually walk in the door for the interview. Tell yourself that it's okay, it's normal to feel a little nervous, but hey -- you've gotten this far, right? Your résumé was a hit and that's why you were called in for a job interview, so channel your inner rock star and walk into that room with confidence!

Chapter 11: Getting To Know You

These questions are usually asked at the start of the interview and give the interviewer a general picture of who you are as a career person.

Tell Us About Yourself

This is probably the first question that'll be thrown your way. Take note, however, this is not a license or a cue for you to present a litany of the story of your entire life. It's also not an opportunity to discuss in exhaustive detail every item in your resume, including your birthday and contact number! Consider your answer to this question as a great opportunity to make a successful first pitch to the interviewer why you're probably the right person for the position.

A very good template to use when answering this question is the now-before-tomorrow pattern. As the name suggests, this guide lets you begin your answer about who or where you're at before transitioning to your past – giving information about your previous work experiences and skills. To end your answer to this question, tell the interviewer what you're looking forward to the most in terms of the opportunity within the company.

So how does such an answer look like?

Interviewer:So, Mr./Ms. Tanner, tell me a bit about you.

You:Well, right now, I'm a financial advisor for Solar Life of Africa, where I'm handling the company's top 100 to 150 clients. Previously, I was connected with Acorn International Group (AIG), another major international insurance company, where I generated high net worth leads for the company's sales and marketing division for the first 7 years of my career. I enjoyed the time I spent with AIG and my current work at Solar Life. I'd consider it a great career growth opportunity to go much deeper – handle the top 100 clients – with another major international insurance company. And that's why I'm excited about this opportunity with your company.

Remember to keep the perspective of the company in mind – as discussed in Chapter 2 – when giving your answer. In particular, focus on the characteristics, skills, and experiences you think may be the most relevant for the recruitment manager or the interviewer for helping the company fill the position you're applying for.

Last, try to loosen up by inserting anecdotes or stories that will give the interviewer more information or insights about you. He or she already has your resume, and he or she already knows much of the professional information about you. Personal stories can shed more light on your personality and help them like you as a person and a candidate.

What Are Your Strengths?

While simple and easy to answer, this question could be a disqualifier. Try to think about the reason behind this question. They are wondering how you see yourself and if you have an accurate picture of yourself. This question uncovers self-awareness and provides more insight into personality.

Often, I've interviewed candidates who self-proclaimed their excellence in almost every skill, but when I asked them to give a specific example of HOW they utilized that strength, they stayed general and could not articulate an example. Identify your key strengths and then write out an example or explanation of WHY you know it is a strength.

How to Identify Your Key Strengths

The first step in identifying your strengths is to brainstorm. List all the strengths you can think of on a piece of paper. Think of at least 10 and be creative. This isn't the time to be "modest" or "humble." Don't edit at this stage; just write. You'll have time to remove irrelevant or insignificant strengths later. Key strengths can include work experience, career track record, skills, talents, soft skills, educational achievements, certifications earned, and relevant trainings attended.

Now that you've created your initial list of key strengths, it's time to narrow it down and focus on the top 5. Rank your identified strengths first by importance or significance to the job at-hand then according to your ability to discuss them comfortably during the interview. Pick the top 5 most important that you can comfortably discuss or learn to discuss during interviews. Having 5 options ensures you have more than enough, and chances are, you won't be able to go through all 5. It's better to have more than less!

To choose the best of your best key strengths for job interviews, one thing you must remember is accuracy. Keep it real! Don't "borrow" the strengths of other people to impress their interviewers. Don't exaggerate your key strengths. If you're able to sell an average of $10,000 worth of merchandise every month, don't inflate it to $50,000! It may work in the short-term, but it's not how to build a long-term career. Stick to your integrity, and when it's a great fit, you will win the job.

When identifying your strengths, you must also be specific. So instead of saying you have a pleasing personality, which is too general, go with a more specific aspect of a pleasing personality, such as the ability to make people you just met feel greatly at ease with you, or you're able to make even the seemingly mute (extremely shy) people talk about themselves within a few minutes of talking to you. Don't be generic. If practically all your colleagues can lay claim to the key strengths you identified, then it may be too generic and not worth including in your list.

Humility shouldn't be applied when brainstorming for your key strengths. Arrogance shouldn't be either. Be confident – if you really have them, tell about them! Remember, your interviewer won't be putting modesty at the top of the list of qualifications for the position you're applying for. Instead, confidence would be one of those at the top, so if you show confidence during the interview, it's a good time to start, even before the interview happens.

Once you're done shortlisting your list of key strengths, try to think of one real example or story you can give or tell during the interview that showcases each of the top 5 strengths you shortlisted. Why do this? It's because rattling off a list of your greatest attributes won't mean much unless the interviewers can get a clear picture of how those could relate to the position at-hand and how those could be beneficial for the organization. Examples or stories provide the bridge that connects your key strengths to the company you're applying in.

Keep the stories short, simple, and straight to the point. Ideally, each example or story should be only a couple of minutes. Take the time to practice sharing those examples or stories in advance, so you sound natural and confident in the actual interviews.

Pitfalls to Watch Out for When Discussing Your Strengths

It may seem like this question is a lay-up. Isn't it an open opportunity – a license if you will – to ditch humble pie and brag about your best qualities, where bragging can get you rewarded?

It's this mentality that has been the pitfall for many interviewees who have sat in the seat across from me. Be mindful of who you really are… have an accurate view of yourself in the mirror. Have awareness of your strengths, weaknesses, and careers. Take the time to reflect on your career and what you really want to accomplish. Ask for feedback from work colleagues and bosses, both former and current. They're in the best and most objective position to give you such information about yourself.

Humility is another common mistake job applicants make when answering this question. Again, this isn't the time to be modest, but neither this is the time to be arrogant or excessive in self-praise. Be confident enough to say what you know you're good at, but keep it real and accurate.

Winning answer:

Since I was young, I've needed to be organized. My room was always neat, my homework always legible and on time, and that has carried on into my work life. I received continuous praise for my ability to manage projects in an organized and timely fashion. I clearly understand the vision for each project, and I use my organizational skills to manage the process through precise calendaring, delegation, and frequent check points. An example of this was when I was the Project Manager for the roll out of some training to the entire organization. I interviewed the primary stakeholders to understand the vision and the deadline. I created a project plan and confirmed the plan with the stakeholders. I worked closely with my team by being specific in assigning their tasks relative to their strengths, and then I measured our success frequently to make sure we were on time. We had to make a few corrections along the way, but my strong organizational skill set kept us on track.

What Are Your Weaknesses?

This is probably one of the most difficult or complex questions to answer in job interviews. One thing you must remember is it's crucial not to gloss over or lie about your answers to this question. Truth is, the reason employers ask this is because they know they can never hire a perfect candidate. They'd rather hire people who are aware of their weaknesses. If a candidate knows what they need to work on, they are more coachable and willing to learn.

What's the best way to answer this tricky question? While there's no magic bullet, a very good way to go about this is to reflect on one thing with which you struggle. It could be detail orientation or inability to delegate tasks. Think of these things from a retroactive perspective, i.e., it's a thing of the past. Tell your interviewer the steps you have taken or are taking to make you much better at those things, and at the moment, you continue to work at becoming even better at them.

Winning answer:

In the past, I was bad at giving presentations in front of an audience, especially those I didn't know personally. When presenting reports in university, I'd be a nervous wreck every time, to the point I'd get a grade that's barely passing.

I didn't let that stop or discourage me. Instead, I took baby steps toward becoming an excellent presenter and public speaker. One is joining our local Toastmasters Club, which gave me opportunities to practice the art of public speaking with small groups at first, which grew in size over many months and years. Another baby step I took was to read books and watch videos on how to become a very good public speaker and presenter.

These days, I still get nervous before I take to the stage and give presentations to hundreds of people at a time. The difference, however, is my audiences tell me I give great talks and presentations, despite being nervous! I still believe I have a long way to go; that's why I continue to be a part of the Toastmasters Club and read materials that help to become a much better public speaker.

Another Winning Answer:

Well, I've heard people say your greatest strength can also be your greatest weakness. As a manager, my teams have always loved me. I have always been focused on creating a family type atmosphere. The problem I've had in the past is that I was so centered on being a family I shied away from giving critical and difficult feedback.

I found that people on my team were not getting promoted as quickly as others on different teams. That bothered me. I wanted the best for the people on my team. I didn't know what I was doing wrong. I went to my mentor, and we reviewed how I work with my team. She helped me to identify this "avoidance" of giving the tough message. I didn't even realize I was doing it. She gave me some suggestions and coached me through it until I learned that I could still care and still have difficult conversations. If I really cared, I owed it to them to have difficult conversations, because it would help them grow.

You might say I have a bleeding heart, because it is still difficult for me to give tough feedback. The difference is that, now, I know it is tough for me. I prepare, I role-play with a mentor or peer, and I anticipate all potential scenarios. Since I've used this process, I've had 8 of my 12 team members get promoted. That is more than any other team in the past year. They are learning better, because I am challenging myself to be better for each of them.

These answers demonstrate self-awareness, willingness to learn and be coached, humility, and growth. Be real, honest, and vulnerable. Your interviewer will trust you if you can help them see you know you can always be better.

What Can You Offer Us That Someone Else Cannot? OR Why Should We Hire You?

Hiring managers normally ask this question to find out particular aspects of your character. The way you answer this question will give your interviewer a sneak peek into what your personal values are and your ability to evaluate yourself properly. The best way to answer this is to look at the things that set you apart or make you unique.

Focus on answering with factual confidence. Speak of your skills that make you a good fit and discuss any extraordinary results you have experienced because of your background or your implementation of a process.

Chapter 12: Optimizing Your Resume And Cover Letter To Stand Out

THE APPLICANT TRACKING SYSTEMS

1. Avoid spelling mistakes

Whether your resume is being looked at by a human or a machine, spelling mistakes make you look like a poor candidate. However, spelling mistakes are far more costly when you're sending your resume to an Applicant tracking systems (ATS), rather than a recruiter or hiring manager. While humans can empathize, and even forgive a spelling mistake, applicant tracking systems cannot.

Applicant tracking systems rank candidates by the number of keywords on their resume that match the job description or a search query being run by the recruiter. If you misspell even just one word on your resume, it can prevent you from appearing in the search results or cause your resume to fall in the ranking. Have a proofreader check your resume for spelling mistakes before you begin applying for jobs.

2. Keep the appearance simple

Less is not always more but when it comes to optimizing your resume for ATS, the less unnecessarily fancy your resume is, the higher the chances are of your resume being correctly parsed by an applicant tracking systems. ATS can be easily confused by pictures, fancy characters, typefaces and even formatting, preventing you from appearing in keyword searches. The ATS is most likely to parse and store your resume correctly if you stick to a standard resume format, font and file type. ATS-friendly resumes are typically chronologically formatted, size eleven or twelve font, written in a simple typeface (such as Times New Roman or Arial), and saved into a .pdf or .docx file. Opts for a simple, standard resume for any applications you submit online.

3. Match your resume keywords

A resume without the correct keywords will automatically exclude you from the running every time. Applicant tracking systems rely heavily on screening the content of resumes to identify the best-matched applicants. To ensure your resume ranks well in the ATS, match the keywords on your resume to those listed on the job description. Then, when a recruiter runs a keyword search to quickly sift through the candidates in their database, the ATS will find that your resume contains the same keywords and pull up your profile for review. While you can manually match the keyword on a job description against your resume, it can be a lengthy process and cause you to miss key terms.

A resume optimizing tool can compare your resume against the job description and instantly generate a list of the terms that appear on the job description but are missing from your resume.

4. Tailor your application for each job

No two resumes or cover letters you submit should ever be the same. Each time you submit your application for a position, tailor it to the exact job you are applying for. Each job description is likely to be worded slightly differently, requiring you to re-write parts of your resume to match the wording of the job description. You can even save time by starting with a standard "template" resume and tailoring it each time you submit a job application. Simply optimizing your resume keywords for one job and then sending out that same resume for similar positions is unlikely to yield the desired results. If you really want to stand out, submitting a well structured and tailored resume is also important. Starting with a cover letter template designed to optimize keywords and highlight your accomplishments can also help you rank more highly in the ATS and get a step up on your competition

OPTIMIZE YOUR RESUME AND COVER LETTER

2. USING KEYWORDS- KEYWORD OPTIMIZATION

1. Selecting keywords

Certain words are crucial to include ensuring that your resume does not go unnoticed by the computer software that is programmed to parse for specific skills and merits.

The first thing you can do is evaluate what you have done in your career. Recall all of the experience that you have, maybe something that you have forgotten about is incredibly relevant to the job you're applying for. Do some research. Make sure that you are aware of all of the terminology in your field. From specialized certification to standard training, be aware of how things are commonly phrased and make sure they appear using keyword optimization for your resume and cover letter. Also, don't neglect the information given to you in the job posting! Most of the time the job listing spells out exactly what requirements the employer is looking for; it wouldn't hurt to include the same keywords used in the listing.

2. Avoid keyword stuffing

One of the most beneficial things that you can do to prepare your resume is to place the most important words towards the top of each section but also dispersed throughout in an even and logical fashion.

Don't fall into the common "keyword stuffing" trap.

Just because you have words that you need to include doesn't mean that you can simply throw them into your writing with no sort of rhyme or reason. Do not oversell yourself by including too many keywords. This can be a red flag to a computer program as well as an employer because it will look as though you do not know how to write a resume or cover letter correctly. Evenly disperse important phrases to emphasize them just enough.

2. Make them count

Each situation and job application is different, and there are a variety of factors that have an effect on which words you should include. This is why keyword optimization for your resume and cover letter is such a noteworthy topic to not only make your resume stand out in a technological screening process but make you appear more focused and qualified for the position that you are applying for.

What Now?

There are a few additional elements that you can employ to ensure that the keyword optimization for your resume and cover letter is effective. Utilize action verbs to further embellish your writing and appear more impressive. Also, exhaust all of your resources to ensure that you have the perfect resume and cover letter. You can also use them on your social media profiles.

Chapter 13: What Your Body Says About You

"Only those who dare to fail greatly can ever achieve greatly."——Robert F.Kennedy

You may think that you're the calmest and most composed person ever, but your body language CAN say otherwise! It's a good thing to be aware of your body language as soon as you step into the lobby of your potential new work place, maybe even before you get to the lobby. You never know who you're walking across the parking lot or sharing the elevator with, be polite and give everyone a warm smile. A good percentage of hiring managers admit to asking their receptionists their opinions on potential candidates. Studies show that a whopping seventy percent of surveyed hiring managers say they can spot the right candidate for a position within thirty seconds of interaction, this could be due to your dressing but a lot of that can also be attributed to body language. From shaking hands to nervous twitches, anything your limbs decide to do at the worst possible moment can have the tendency to either enhance or ruin your chances of clinching your dream job. However, you can avoid those embarrassing scenes by keeping a few things in mind as you're called in for your interview:

The All Important Handshake

Ah yes, the famous handshake. They can be used in a number of different rituals, but did you know that the level of pressure you use can have a number of different meanings?

Do's and Don'ts of the handshake ritual

Don't panic! Many people dread shaking hands since it's the first direct contact they have with their potential employers. It'll only takes a few seconds but the handshake has the potential to tell an employer the finer details of your personality that you probably left out of your resume. If you have sweaty palms, for instance, then you can probably say goodbye to that position you had your eye on. WIPE THEM OFF before you are shown into the room for the interview. Interviewers will instantly know that you're very nervous and it won't look good for you especially if the position requires a strong-willed employee. Well, that would narrow your options quite a bit, not many positions of value require a patsy.

But what if you're called before you've had time to do it out of sight of any curious onlookers? No worries, that's an easy one to handle. Just casually run your hands down your shirt as if you were ironing out any creases. Better yet, just rest your right hand on your leg while waiting and say goodbye to those wet palms!

Word to the wise, whatever you do, don't wipe your hands when it's time for the handshake. The interviewer will only believe you have low self-esteem. However, this scenario won't be as bad as wiping them off after they shake your hand. Even if it has a trace of mustard on it, Never reach for that Kleenex! It's the ultimate insult.

Then we have the 'dead fish' grip. You know the one where you let your hand go all floppy and lifeless? Don't do that! This will instantly be seen as low self esteem on your part. In fact, you might be leaving the impression that you're not comfortable shaking hands at all! In many cultures a man or woman who won't shake hands is not trustworthy enough to work with. Again, doing the opposite is a bad idea as well. Gripping your interviewer's hand as if you're trying to crush it will only be annoying apart from inflicting pain that will certainly not be appreciated. You can come across as being too aggressive and forceful as well.

Your best bet would be to take your lead from the interviewer. If you're given a strong grip, then tailor yours to match its intensity and firmness. If the interviewer seems a bit elderly, then please do try to be a bit gentle. You'll only come across as being over confident and insensitive if you squeeze too hard.

Now here's the recipe for the Perfect Handshake. Yes, there is one. All you have to do is grasp his/her hand palm to palm and match the amount of pressure they're using (as mentioned before). Count to 3, release, and follow it up with a genuine smile, while maintaining eye contact all through the process. Now, that's a handshake that elicits trust and confidence.

The Eyes Reveal All!

They say that eyes are the windows to the soul. You might not be surprised to learn this saying is key to your chances of success at job interviews as well. Making the right amount of eye contact can speak volumes about your capabilities and your confidence levels. It can even tell the interviewer how much you trust him/her. It can reveal how truthful you are at that time.

Maintaining eye contact will help you figure out whether the person meeting you actually understands what you're saying or not. If they space out for instance, try and tone down that speech you prepared. No one likes a blabbermouth anyway.

Your 'poker face' will help you here! The more open your face is, the more comfortable you'll make the interviewer. Employers will be more willing to hire you if they know you're an easy going person, since it'll also mean that you're a team oriented person. Plus you'll seem more polite if you keep at it. If you keep shifting your eyes, on the other hand, employers may think you're either too nervous or you're not being truthful.

There are 2 ways of getting the perfect eye contact according to the situation you find yourself in; as a listener and as a speaker. If you're listening to your (hopefully) future employer, you need to make a lot more eye contact. Not too much that it makes it seem you're staring but just enough to convey your genuine interest. There is a fine line to these things. It makes sense if you think about it. The speaker will appreciate your qualities more if you seem like you're making a genuine effort to capture the essence of every word they're saying.

When the time comes for you to speak, on the other hand, then your best bet will be to keep eye contact to a minimum. Keep staring at them for too long and they may think you have a serious problem, if you know what I mean. About 5 to 10 seconds is enough to connect with the interviewer. Reduce the time after that to lower the intensity of your gaze so that they don't think you're trying to start a staring match. Remember, maintaining eye contact will help you get that flow you desperately need for a good rapport to develop. The situation may even turn against you if the employer thinks that you're trying to have a battle of wills or are trying to be too familiar! Shifting your gaze is okay, but only if you bring it back just as quickly. And in a panel interview scenario, be sure to meet every panelist's eye confidently, while focusing on whoever asked the question you're in the process of answering.

Good Posture Speaks Louder Than Job Interview Answers

Believe it or not, most interviewers can figure out the type of person you are just by observing you on that hot seat! The way you sit says a lot about your character and can also speak volumes about the way you think. However, being too conscious of the way you present yourself may result in quite a few blunders on your part.

The good news is that it doesn't take much to achieve that correct posture. The first thing you have to learn is to keep your hands, arms and elbows to yourself. Keep them off the desk if there is one in front of you and try to keep them below your interviewer's gaze. Don't stare at your hands if you have no idea what to do with them!

Sitting straight is a very good habit to practice. A 'strong backbone' has the ability to make you seem confident and attentive at the same time, while a slumped one can make you seem bored and thus, disrespectful. Try not to lean back on that comfy sofa you were ushered into; it's a trap designed to lull you to sleep and let you put down your guard! A posture like that may communicate that you like talking about yourself more than listening to the interviewer. It might simply be understood as you really not wanting to be there or you simply being uninterested.

The best sitting posture would be to sit up straight while leaning slightly forward in your seat. Imagine the top of your head being connected to the ceiling with a piece of string. This is a non-verbal way to say that you're interested in what your interviewer is trying to say. Try and keep your feet on the floor instead of crossing them if you're in full view since it might come off as an informal posture. It will also prevent your feet from jiggling or from tapping on the floor, which is also a sign of nervousness. The upright posture will also reveal your chest, chin and neck area which is an unconscious show of openness, trust and honesty. It's your way of saying "I have nothing to hide."

You're allowed to move about a bit in your chair if you want to get rid of any stiffness in your body after sitting still for so long.

Relaxing your shoulders is also a good idea, but not enough that you start to slump forward! Place your hands on the armrests (if there are any) or on your lap so that you can use them to make a point more interesting if you're inclined to do so. Interviewers are more impressed with people who are expressive with their hands and often see it as a sign of confidence in your abilities. But try not to get overexcited by flailing those arms all over the place. Short of seeming crazy, you might come across as being over-confident if you're not careful.

Make nerves work for you

Being nervous isn't just about feeling anxious; it's a serious problem for many. Some people experience full out panic attacks during interviews, while others are lucky enough to be able to deal with it a lot better. Nervousness has the ability to make your knees go weak, your throat dry up, and your bowels to loosen in a typical fight or flight primeval instinct reaction.

A panic attack at that moment can seriously reduce your chances of making a 'sane' impression on the interviewer. Let's face it, no one is going to hire you if you can't stop your hands shaking or teeth chattering long enough to give a reasonable answer! In the event of a panic attack, take the time to take deep breaths and repeat to yourself "I can do this, I can do this". Just hope the panic attack doesn't happen in the presence of your interviewer, muttering incoherently under your isn't exactly a recipe that will snag you a hefty employment contract.

It may seem like just another thing you have to think about in an already stressful situation, but keeping those nerves in check can help you answer those interview questions easily and with a lot more sincerity. The good news is that nerves CAN be controlled and can even be channeled into an unconscious positive effort on your part!

Thought vs. Emotions in a Job Interview Scenario

Think about it. Is it really your emotions that make your knees buckle whenever you think of that upcoming interview?

The thing is, the problem lies more in what you're thinking at the moment rather than what you're feeling or what you're actually experiencing. If you're in a situation that makes you scared for instance, the emotion generated will be fear. If the thought running through your mind is whether or not you might get the job, then you might be feeling nervous or anxious. Similarly a sense of hopelessness might set in if you think you didn't do well or you're not going to do well.

See? The thoughts running through your head are what impact the emotions you feel at the moment. Anyone who feels too anxious or too scared will obviously have a hard time functioning in normal situations, let alone a job interview. However, this provides a good chance for you to nip this problem in the bud! In other words, get rid of the unwanted thoughts and you'll get rid of those unwanted emotions like fear and anxiety, it's not going to be easy but it's a battle you can definitely win. The trick to it is replacing the negative emotions with positive emotions that generate peace and calm. Your mind can't stay empty it has to be filled with some thoughts. Why not make them positive?

Just think happy thoughts in the meanwhile (I can do this! This is a piece of cake!) You'll do just fine.

If the thoughts that grow the fear and anxiety in your mind are scenes where you walk into the room and the interviewer is grim, unfriendly, and that triggers your insecurity so you say all the wrong things, or you picture yourself walking out dejected after what you think is a terrible meeting. Don't worry about it, it's okay. The good thing is we have the power to change our thoughts and even more important, we can change our emotions by consciously making the effort to do so. Instead of visualizing the worst case scenarios, simply think of all the good things that can happen in that interview scenario, you walk in and the interviewer is friendly and has a genuine interest in you. You're asked all the questions that you know like the back of your hand and can answer with expertise. The interviewer is so impressed that they offer you the job on the spot. They ask you when you would like to start at the job. You cancel all the negative, fear inducing thoughts with more positive happy thoughts.

Remember, the more you practice this technique, the better your chances of making a huge impression in that question and answer session. Accept as many interview invitations as you can for posterity's sake. Record each interview on your phone (there are several apps for that purpose), be sure to keep it well hidden in your pocket and critique yourself afterwards, note the things you did or said wrong and areas you could have been better, there's no greater teacher than experience. This will allow you to hone your skills and manage your nerves so that you can do better next time on subsequent interviews.

Here's a summary of body language do's and don'ts in an interview Scenario:

If you're being led into the interview room, even if you know where it is, never take the lead. Follow the person assigned to direct you.

Never take a seat before being invited to do so

Be sure to give the "perfect handshake" and have a genuine smile on your face when you do so. or like my grandma would say, "Smile with your eyes".

Make and hold eye contact when shaking hands and when making a point or responding to a question. When in a panel interview hold each individual's gaze for a little and go back to the person being addressed or responded to directly.

If you're the type that makes a point with a lot of hand movements you have to be careful with your motions. Too much of pointing can come across as being overly aggressive. Chopping motions would also necessarily come across as too combative. If you must use hand gestures be sure to keep your hands above the table but below your shoulder level. Anything above the level of your shoulders would make you appear frantic

Never rub or touch your nose during the interview. It's seen as a sign of dishonesty while it is just offensive to some people

Avoid rubbing the back of your head or neck. It makes you seem uninterested.

Do not sit with your arms folded across your chest. It is seen as being guarded, defensive and unfriendly

Be sure to not cross your legs while shaking one over the other. It's a sign of boredom

Show interest in the interview and conversations by keeping an interested expression at all times. Nod moderately to convey your interest.

Ensure you establish a zone of personal comfort between yourself and the interviewer. People feel uncomfortable when personal space is invaded and an interview scenario is no different. Sit about one and a half feet from your interviewer.

Body Language Cues that signify Interview Success

Just like body language can point the interviewer to your hidden strengths and weakness, it can also reveal a lot about your interviewer. You can tell the way the interview is going and if you might need to do crank up your efforts at making a good impression on the interviewer. There are also body language cues that can give you a good idea of the kind of impression you've made on the interviewer. Here are some signs that can tell you if you need to turn up the style or you already have the interview in the bag

Watch the feet

If an interviewer's feet are pointed unnaturally away from you towards the door that's a bad sign. Even if the words being said are at odds with the body language cues you need to regain their interest. If the feet are crossed and pointed forward toward you then you might just be on the right track!

Mirrored gestures

Just like on a date when two people find mutual enjoyment from a conversation, they start to unconsciously mirror the other's gestures. A mirroring of gestures shows engagement and interest from both parties. If you see this often then you're more likely to be in high regard with your interviewer, keep doing what you've been doing up till then and you might just cross the finish line in first place ahead of the raging horde of competitors.

Watch eye contact

The more eye contact an interviewer gives to you, the more the chance they're interested in giving you the job. Human nature tends to ensure that we stare longer at things or people we like more than those we don't.

Chapter 14: Person Job Searches As Potential Interviews

On the spot interviews are not very common, but there is always that possibility, especially in the retail sector and with small companies. Don't go out looking shabby dressed in jeans or shorts with your children tagging along unless your sole purpose is to pick up applications to take home and fill out before returning. But you might miss an opportunity for an interview on that day when the store manager is likely to be on site.

Certainly if you just happen to walk into a store that has a help wanted sign you are not going to make a special trip back to the business to pick up an application, but this is not your ordinary course of action nor is it one that you should do on a consistent basis. However, if you go out with the sole intent to look for employment, dress appropriately and leave the children with a sitter in case the company does on the spot interviews. You do not want to sabotage your chances of being hired because you failed to plan accordingly. Of course, during the Christmas season it is very common for retail businesses to leave applications in plain sight where job seekers can pick one up, take it home and bring it back later. You do want to be certain when you return with the application you are prepared for the possibility of an on the site interview.

Bringing a friend with you when you are job searching is not recommended; unless the friend is providing transportation or also job searching. In the case of a friend providing transportation, there is no need for the friend to go inside with you, so you might want to ask your meet to meet you at a nearby coffee shop or similar establishment. You may do so when those friends are also seeking employment. Do not treat it as any more than a job search; do not make it a point to tell the company you have a friend or relative with you who is also seeking employment. This also falls into the category of too much personal chitchat and should be avoided.

Interviewing With Multiple People

Some companies will choose to have an applicant interview with more than one person at the same time instead of having two separate interviews. It saves time for both for them and the applicant. This is a good way for the department heads where everyone can come together and ask their own questions of the applicant at the same time. It also saves the applicant from having to return for another interview if they are qualified for the position. It should be easy for Human Resources to review the qualifications of each application and determine which people who best suit the requirements of the department. Interviewing with multiple interviewers will give each person an opportunity to ask questions without repeating the same ones as is the case when applicants meet individually with each person who is a part of the hiring process.

Are interviews involving more than one interviewer effective? Should the applicant be able to interview with each person individually? For the applicant who is taking time from another job for the interview, it saves time when they can meet all of the decision makers all at one time. This also saves time for the company because they do not have to schedule many interviews with different people different times. It will also shorten the length of the selection process because what is normally two is three steps is now reduced to one.

This type of interview is practical for both small and large companies; though corporations are more likely to use this method of interviewing. This type of interview might be uncomfortable or intimidating for some applicants, they must consider the fact they will meet with all of these same people at some point during the interviewing process, but this will actually be more efficient and preferable to meeting with Human Resources, asked to stay longer or come back at another time to meet with the department heads that will be actually making the selection. In the total scheme of things it is much easier to meet with everyone at the same time instead of having to come back or stay longer than you had originally planned.

Keys to a Successful Interview

Having a successful interview goes beyond simply looking presentable and showing the interviewer you have the right qualifications for the job. It does not guarantee you will be hired for the job. The key to being hired is selling yourself to the interviewer, and that means you have to go beyond proving the extent of your impeccable skills. Do not be over confident—the most qualified applicant can lose a potential position because he or she possessed poor interviewing skills.

One of the worst mistakes someone can make is to apply for a job for which they are not qualified and try to convince the interviewer they have the skills to perform the job. Even if you think you are the most trainable person in the world, if a company says they want someone with experience you had better either have the experience or be able to learn it quickly. No matter how qualified you may be if you do not project the right personal image you will not be hired. Many young people fail to understand this because they do not accept the advice of others concerning proper dress code for an interview. The problem is sometimes that if it is their first job they do not own anything else, but if you want to be hired you need to buy proper clothes for interviews. Most restaurants and many retail outlets may not care; many other businesses will certainly reject your application based on the way you dress when you come for an interview. Dressed professionally or at least business casual attire and arrive on time. In the case you are going to be late because of circumstances beyond your control, call and let the interviewer know and give them the option of still seeing you or rescheduling the interview.

Preparation

Even if you are going to interview for another job, there are some things you can do to prepare for the interview. If you are looking for a career change, especially one that will mean an increase in salary and/or benefits, you want to make a good impression on the potential employer. If you are coming from another interview that is more casual, make sure you have a change of clothing to fit the protocol of the next company you are going for an interview

Even if you have mailed, emailed or faxed a copy of your resume it is a good idea to bring a copy with you. An interviewer often will ask questions concerning information on your resume, and it is much easier for you if you have a copy of your resume with you. Do not attempt to remember everything that is on your resume especially if you have a lengthy professional career. Attempting and failing to recall dates and events that are on your resume may make you appear unprofessional and unprepared for the interview. More often than not, many interviewers want a fresh copy of your resume as they usually made all kinds of notes on the copy you have previously sent and would like a fresh copy to view during the interview.

Make sure to choose your clothing the night before the interview so that you have enough time to make sure they are appropriate and press anything that may be wrinkled. Be careful of the colors you choose—choosing bright colors may take attention away from you. Stick to solid dark shades and choose styles that are conservative and not too revealing. Although this applies more to women than men do, it is a point that is worth repeating. You want the interviewer to look at you and not at your cleavage.

Have a notebook and pen to take notes. There will be some points you will want to recall for later such as working hours, rules and regulations and especially the interviewer's name so that you can send a "thank you" note.

Chapter 15: Before The Interview

Do Your Homework

Look at the preparation the same way as you would study for a test. Because an interview really is a kind of test and the grade you get might determine whether you go further in the process or not.

Find out everything you can about the company. How big they are, where their offices are located, how many people they employ and even who their CEO is. (That's a common interview question!)

But even take it further and research their competition as well. Find out who they compete with in the marketplace and why they are better or worse than the others. This can help you better position yourself and your skills. Do your best to get acquainted with as much of the overall industry as you possibly can.

Write down statistics such as last year's sales, stock prices, industry sales number of employees and other specifics that might be able to be worked into answers to questions to showcase your knowledge about the company and where it stands in the industry.

Understand the Company and its Wants and Needs

Try and determine the needs and wants of the company as well. What is it they wish to accomplish? Are they looking to grow or are they already expanding. What are the main problems with the company? What is the company looking for in its employees? What does the company place a high value on as far as employees are concerned? What does the company need to move forward?

All of this information can be used to determine how to best represent yourself in the interview. It will allow you to determine how to give them more of what they want and how to make them feel that you are the answer to their needs and problems.

Be a Problem Solver

Speaking of problems, every employee exists to address or resolve a problem. Job responsibilities are designed to make sure that certain things happen so certain problems don't occur. Engineers design safe and durable products so those problems do not occur. Sales people make sure products are represented well and properly so they sell very well. Every position is there to address or solve a problem and you need to understand what those problems really are.

During the interview it is up to you to let them know how you can solve particular problems and why you are the best person to solve those problems. You can bring up specific skills, accomplishments and experience that will all help you become very effective at exactly what it is the company needs from you. Though they might not see it that way if hiring you to fill the impression will make those problems go away then you have a good shot at landing the job.

Connecting the Dots

Hopefully in your resumes you helped make direct connections between your education and experience and what the company is looking for from an applicant.

If you have already done this, that's great! If not, you need to start doing it now! You must not leave it up to other to make these connections, you must take it upon yourself to make sure they understand all that you bring to the table and how it relates to them!

This is sort of like those "connecting the dots" drawings and puzzles some of us did as kids. You know the ones I'm talking about. The ones where you draw lines between numbers. The more numbers you connect the clearer the picture becomes. This is exactly what you must do regarding your education and accomplishments.

You need to take every qualification and need and then connect it to something you have accomplished or know about. The more direct connections you can make tying your qualifications and achievements to specific things they are looking for the more relevant you will become to them. This is where and how you can separate yourself from the rest of the applicants.

Think about all of this just like creating that line drawing connecting the dots. As you make yourself more relevant you help create a picture in the mind of the interviewer seeing you in the position and doing a great job. Though the person doesn't actually "see" the picture it forms a powerful impression one the less.

The less you leave to chance the more accurately your "story" will be told to the interviewer. The more "dots" you connect the clearer the picture, the greater the message and the less confusion you will have. All of these are very good for you to have in an interview.

Prepare a List of Likely Questions

Interviews are not one way with the interviewer asking you questions and you answering them. Sometimes they will ask you what questions you might have to ask them. This can be a great way for you to steer the conversation over to something that is one of your stronger areas and away from your weaknesses.

Prepare questions that will easily lead the conversation to something that you are very good at or have several accomplishments with. Or maybe you have specific knowledge about something most other people don't have. You can then ask a question that will lead into that topic. This allows you to get information about yourself to the interviewer without being obvious and without interrupting the flow of the interview.

Having questions prepared also shows that you put some thought in the interview and that you really do have some interest in the job and the company. It shows initiative and it shows commitment. That is one of the reasons interviewers ask if you have any questions. They want to see if you have really looked into this opportunity. Whatever you do, don't just say "No, you have covered everything. I'm good!"

Google Yourself

Not many people think of doing this but it can be a very important and eye-opening thing to do.

As you know, the internet contains a wealth of information about everything and sometimes every one. These days just about every company will do an internet search under the same of the applicant especially when they get into the latter stages of the process. Doing a search yourself might help you deal with things they might find. It might also make you aware of what you should or should not do in the future as well.

Many of us are not aware that any time we post a comment or a picture or whenever our name appears in any document or post that it becomes searchable by the search engines. So those drunken Spring Break phots back in College? They're there for the world to see! The comments on Face book? Searchable. The rants on those propaganda websites? Searchable. Those comments you made in anger and then instantly regretted? Searchable.

While it might be possible to get these items removed, it is not an easy process. With freedom of speech also comes freedom to do stupid stuff as well. The only think you might try to do is make a lot of positive comments, post a lot of positive articles and just get your name out there as much as possible in a positive manner. This might push some of those regrettable things further back in the rankings and the company might not go back that many pages.

But the best thing is not to post anything like that in the first place.

But whether or not there is anything bad out there it is best to find out about it now so you can address it openly and honestly if asked about it. Whether you are looking for a job or not it is a good practice to check under you name at least once or twice a year. This can alert you to several things like identity theft.

Interview Yourself or Have Someone Interview You

"Mock" interviews or interviews given to you by other people for practice can be a great way to gain experience and refine your answers to certain questions. Chances are someone else will be tougher on you than you would be on yourself so it is a more realistic experience than it would have been doing it yourself.

Pick out all the questions that you feel you are likely to be asked and also give the person interviewing you the ability to throw in a few other ones as well just to keep you on your toes and thinking right.

As far as your role in concerned, try and treat this as an actual interview. That means no stopping to think or stopping in mid answer to go back and start over. You can do multiple interview to help you get more comfortable but as each one is going on, treat it as the real deal.

Tell the person interviewing you to not go easy on you either. The real interviewer isn't and neither should the practice person. If possible, get someone experienced in either the industry you are applying in or someone with Human Resource experience that knows how real interviews are done.

Practice

As you go through the practice stage, stop yourself and go over anything that you do not feel confident in. Be honest with yourself and don't tell yourself that you did well when you know you didn't. Just keep practicing things until they become second nature to you. Above all, throughout the entire process, be honest with yourself.

Part of the practice experience is identifying weaknesses and turning them into strengths. If you are not honest with yourself that is most certainly not going to happen.

When Should You Start Practicing?

Ideally, you should start practicing long before you actually have an important interview. Confidence takes time to build. Also, giving yourself the time you need will remove a lot of the pressure from the process. It is hard to practice something right when your interview is at noon time tomorrow!

Give yourself plenty of time to do it and do it right. They say practice makes perfect and while we don't need perfect, we do need pretty close to it!

Chapter 16: Interview Do's And Don'ts

As we continue along our journey to the perfect job interview, in our efforts to attain that sought after perfect new job, there are several important do's and don'ts for interviewing that will greatly guide and assist you during your personal employment interview. Here are some of the most important, and useful tips on the do's and don'ts of job interviewing. Those candidates who give particular attention to these simple rules and guidelines for engaging in a successful job interview are sure to achieve a satisfactory result during this phase of their job-hunting journey.

Critical Do's for the Perfect Interview

1. Dress appropriately for your personal interview. Always err on the side of being conservative, and indeed be certain that your overall personal appearance and grooming is above remarkable.

2. Give extreme attention to your interview time and location, and always allow yourself ample time to find the

office, park your vehicle, walk inside, and perhaps utilize the rest rooms for a last minute freshen up.

3. Be sure to arrive 15 minutes prior to the interview. If the interviewer has requested that you arrive earlier than 15 minutes, be certain to comply with their specific request.

4. Upon your arrival, display the utmost in courtesy and respect to the receptionist or administrative assistant that you encounter first. Remember their thoughts and opinions could be solicited by the interviewer, and can potentially have an impact on whether or not you ultimately get hired.

5. When you enter the interview room, be certain to offer a firm handshake, make direct eye contact as you speak, and present with a pleasant facial expression as you initially greet your interviewer.

6. Listen with intent has your interviewer introduces themselves so you are sure to address them properly throughout the interview process. Remember, even if they provide you with a first and last name,

always address them by title (Mr. Miss, Ms.) unless they specifically advise you to do otherwise.

7. Maintain direct eye contact throughout the entire interview.

8. Be prepared to answer all questions and, if necessary, back up all your comments with specific details and examples. You want to be thorough and concise with all your responses. If you do not understand a question, always ask for clarification.

9. Always be yourself, and provide honest, straightforward responses.

10. Present with a very positive attitude, and show your interviewer that you have a genuine interest in not only the employment opportunity, but also the company itself, and the industry within which it falls.

11. When the opportunity presents itself, ask intelligent questions about the position and the company. This shows the interviewer that you are truly interested, and can indicate that you had conducted

appropriate research on the company beforehand.

12. When the interview appears to be coming to an end, be certain to ask when and from whom you should expect further communications so you are prepared, in advance, for the next step of the hiring process.

13. Once the interview is completed, offer your interviewer a firm handshake yet again, give direct eye contact, and thank him or her for their time and then gracefully leave the room.

Critical Don'ts for the Perfect Interview

1. Never make negative comments about prior employers or others.

2. Never give false responses to questions asked, and certainly do not exaggerate circumstances or details.

3. Do not be unprepared for typical, everyday interview questions.

4. Do not give the implication that you are simply interviewing for this job just for the sake of getting a job, or because of its location; and especially do not imply that

you are interviewing simply because of an interest in the salary range.

5. Never inquire about salary or benefits at a first interview, unless the subject is brought up by your interviewer. These days, interviewer are aware that the salary information is usually freely available when applying for the job. So if you inquire about it during the interview, this may be conceived as lack of attention to detail.

6. Do not give the impression or imply that you are desperate for employment, and are willing to take any job that comes along.

7. Don't give responses that leave your interviewer questioning your position on a topic, and certainly do not leave them feeling doubtful about a response you have given, or the validity of your response.

8. Even if the questions are frustrating to you, and the overall process is more challenging than you anticipated, never show any signs of frustration or negativity.

9. Never call your interviewer by their first name, and in addressing them with title (Ms. Miss Mr.) never assume that a female interviewer is a Miss or a Mrs., always address her as Ms.

10. Never, never, never chew gum during an interview, and absolutely do not attend an interview wreaking of cigarette smoke.

11. Do not allow your cell phone to ring, or a text message to come through while interviewing, and never, ever respond to a call or text message. If your cell phone does go off, be quick to apologize, and turn it off immediately.

12. Finally, never bring anybody with you to your interview. If you opt to do so, certainly you will be looked upon as irresponsible, and incapable of your own independence. This will be extremely detrimental to your interview, and most assuredly a deal breaker for any chance of obtaining the new employment.

Adhering to these very important, and yet practical, do's and don'ts of job interviewing is sure to offer the ideal candidate the wisdom, the know-how, and the confidence needed to deliver a professional, and even convincing interview presentation. In addition, following these simple guidelines will highlight your overall professional and personal ethics, as well as your qualifications and capabilities of being productive, and truly successful in the current position being offered. If you master each of these do's and don'ts days before your interview, certainly you will find yourself a party to a very comfortable, pleasant, and truly professional interviewing experience that can absolutely lead to an attractive job offer.

Chapter 17: Understanding The Salary Or Hourly Pay

"What is your salary expectations?" Know what the pay range consists of before going into the interview. If you managed to avoid the pay question while applying for the job, expect to know it for the interview.

If you are remaining in the same job or similar industry then it can be expected that you know the pay range. When preparing for the salary or hourly rate discussion, consider what you realistically would expect your pay increase to be at your current job. That would be the pay you provide the interviewer.

If you are going to a new position or new industry, then you will need to research the pay range. You can search online using the job title, city or county, the state, and salary for results. If someone lives in Dallas, Texas searching for a customer service manager position, then it would be entered on a search engine such as Google or Bing as "Customer Service Manager Dallas Texas Salary." That person would find multiple web sites listing salary expectations for that particular job title in the Dallas metropolitan area. Make sure you keep your searches in the geographical area closest to you. Someone who works in Seattle, Washington pay would not be the same as a person working in Little Rock, Arkansas.

After you know the pay range for the position, you should be prepared to provide a financial number to the interviewer. One way of not shooting yourself in the foot by providing a low amount or shocking the interviewer with a number higher than the average worker in that field is to answer with a range versus an exact dollar amount. Therefore, once you have viewed the pay range online, you are able to name a range towards the higher end of your salary or hourly expectations. A response would go like this:

Don't be afraid to say the amount. You want to project that you are confident with the amount you are telling the interviewer and confident in the pay you have researched.

Chapter 18: Pre-Interview Essentials

What to Find Out

Before the interview, you should ask several questions that ensure everyone is on the same page with logistics.

Where is your location?

This is something that the interviewer is supposed to tell you, but it's possible that they will forget. The last thing you want is to be scrambling for the interview location the night before the interview. Make sure you know this at least twenty-four hours in advance whenever possible.

What time is the interview?

As with above, this is something the interviewer should tell you when you receive the invitation to interview. However, the interviewer is likely to have several other interviews scheduled that day. It's quite possible that a mistake can be made. After all, we are all human. Make sure you confirm the interview time. You don't want to miss the interview and have to try to find another place in the interviewer's schedule.

What is the best way to get in contact in case of an emergency?
Certain things happen that are out of our control, so you will want to ask the best way to contact them should any problems arise, such as a flat tire, dead battery, sickness, family crisis, and so on.

> **Pants Down Tip**
>
> If you miss the interview because of a miscommunication error, you've just been caught with your pants down.

Dress Code
What to wear and what not to wear to an interview is a widely-debated topic, and while it is often true that it depends on the position and company you are interviewing for, professional and basic is always best. You don't want to wear something too showy or you may come

across as "too good" for this job. Something simple but professional always works best. If you have any doubts, ask the company representative prior to the interview. Here is what we recommend for men and women.

Men:
- Blue or Black Suit
- Dress Slacks
- Button-down shirt
- Black or Brown Shoes
- Clean-shaven
- Properly Trimmed Hair
- Briefcase or Portfolio

Women:
- Dark pantsuit or skirt suit
- Light-colored button-up blouse
- Closed toe shoes
- Minimal make-up
- Minimal jewelry
- Minimal perfume
- Briefcase or Portfolio

When to Arrive (Earlier Than You Think)

One of the worst possible things that you can do is miss the interview or show up late. Take the time to map your route to the interview spot beforehand. You should give yourself plenty of time to arrive before the interview. There are always circumstances outside our control, so you have to prepare for these. For instance, if you are taking a train and it becomes delayed or you are driving and there is an unexpected amount of traffic. Depending on how far away you are from the interview location, you should arrive to the interview location area **at least two hours beforehand**. I say area because you don't want to arrive at the interview spot two hours before, but at least be in the neighborhood. You can find a nearby Starbucks or other coffeehouse and sit inside and review your notes/study sheets. By this time, you should be feeling pretty confident and just browse your notes. You will then want to head over to the interview location roughly a half hour early.

Sleep and Eat
I am sure you've heard it all before, but getting proper sleep the night before and

eating healthy meals are essential for the interview day. Interviews can be a long, tiring process and you need a sufficient amount of energy to get you through it. Failing to get the proper sleep and nutrition will most definitely affect your performance. You should also bring some sort of extra snack to eat before the interview. Here is what we recommend.

> **PantsDown Tip**
>
> It doesn't matter to the interviewer if there are forces outside your control that makes you late. If you show up late, you've just been caught with your pants down

Sleep:
- 6-8 hours the night before

Breakfast:
- High Protein
- High Fiber
- Complex Carbohydrates
- Good Fats

Extra:

- Protein or snack bar for right before or right after the interview

Chapter 19: Presentation And Grooming

Did you know that an interviewer has the discretion of making up his or her mind on a potential employee from as early as the time you set foot into the room and exchange pleasantries through a handshake? To ladies, taking substantial amount of time in front of the mirror might be habitual, but what about men? Presentation refers to appearance, and in this context, how you prepare for an interview is paramount. On the other hand, grooming is a broader aspect of presentation because it takes a look into bits and bytes of enhancing your physical appearance. Essentially, good grooming is a recipe for proper and appealing presentation.

How many times have you turned up for an interview and felt that something was not right with your dress code, shoes, or hairstyle? How did you come to notice it? Well, the way you look in terms of body grooming can either attract people to you or repel them. This is equally true in the case of a job interview. From the time you enter an interview room, you can notice something about your grooming based on how the members of the interviewing panel react. Do they smile and nod appreciatively or look down? Find out next time you attend a job interview, but to this end you know what to do.

Many people believe that getting hired for a job they have applied for is based on being endowed with the requisite skills and knowledge. However, when such people fail to make it through an interview despite their enormous skills, they start to look for scapegoats and even start saying the interviewer or employer was this and that. But did you know that you could have ruined your own chances by not appearing for the interview in the right attire or dress code?

Like it or not, how you look during a job interview is equally as important as your qualifications. An interview schedule is not the time to showcase your taste for fashion and trendy dressing styles. It is a time to look courteous and sharply dressed.

In this chapter, we take a look at how presentation and grooming are part and parcel of the whole process that will see you crush a job interview and annihilate your competitors.

Good grooming is an important first impression

Appearing for an interview is always a stage in the whole process that could change your life forever. That is to say, how you dress will either elicit in your prospective employer an interest in hiring you or simply be a turn off. When dressing for an interview, wearing high-end official attire is not negotiable. You must dress the part. For a lady, dressing scantily would be distracting, and the interview will definitely not favor you. It is important to dress for the occasion because how you dress will be the basis upon which the interviewer will form a first but lasting impression of you. This is something easy and should therefore provide you with the opportunity t0 crush a job interview and consequently annihilate your competitors. Remember that a picture is often said to be worth a thousand words, and there is no way you can change this conventional view of appearance and imagery. You have to look professionally good because a job interview is not a fashion show.

Grooming as a sign of care

For jobs like sales promotion and marketing, the first impression you give will be the one expected of you should you be hired for the job. When companies post job openings on the web or in the local dailies, they are always specific about the attributes they are looking out for in potential recruits. An example is attention to detail. How you dress for a job interview will make this attribute examinable.

People who dress well for a job interview create an impression of attentiveness to detail, while those who could care less about their appearances come off as careless and are never hired. By being well groomed in hairstyles for men, hairdressing for women, and dress code, you come off as someone who not only cares for personal hygiene but is also keen on details.

Good grooming elevates your self-esteem
Self-esteem is a necessary attribute that any employer will be looking for in an interviewee. Through good grooming through appropriate dress code and general appearance, you will be casting an image of confidence, which is a desirable quality any employers look out for in a potential recruit. Employers want to hire people who can present themselves well, and they can judge this from the way you have dressed for an interview. So if you have been taking this lightly, make a good show of it during your next interview, and you could just be hired instantly.
Fundamental tips on grooming for an interview

Here, you would want to ask and answer the question of what you are supposed to do with regards to grooming before an interview. This is as simple as ensuring that your fingernails are well cut and that your hair is neatly cut if you are a gentleman or appropriately styled if you are a lady. An important part of presentation is that you should not chew gum during an interview because this will be irritating and disruptive. Furthermore, have your portfolio folder or briefcase well cleaned. You should also ensure that your shoes and teeth are properly cleaned and that your pockets are emptied so that there is nothing protruding from your clothes.

The clothes that you put on for a job interview, apart from being official attire, should be well ironed to remove any creases that would paint you as careless. Regarding usage of grooming items like body lotions, perfumes, bathing soaps, and deodorants, always ensure you have used them sparingly.

A lot of perfume would not create a friendly atmosphere for an interview because there could be one or two members of the interviewing panel who are allergic to strong scents.

In summary, grooming and presentation are core necessities that arouse in a prospective employer the right or wrong perception of an interviewee. This therefore calls upon you to make efforts to look good, presentable, and positive before you appear for your next interview.

Chapter 20: Sample Interview Questions And Answers

As I mentioned earlier in the book, doing your research and preparing for possible questions that you may encounter during the interview are vital to your success. Of course, I don't recommend that you present a bland, generic response to questions at an interview that you simply read off the Internet, either.

What I recommend is that you spend some time making yourself comfortable with the things that you are likely to get asked during an interview. Think about what a hiring manager is looking for through your response, and what needs to be done to show that you are precisely the right person for the job. Add that personal touch by finding way to subtly highlight your experience and skills through your answers.

Want to find out what exactly you may encounter? Here are some of the most common questions asked during job interviews and how you can shape your answer for each of them:

Tell me something about yourself.

This may seem like something of a simple, innocuous question but is usually the point that almost everyone seems to fail at. Its importance cannot be underestimated. Refrain from giving away every bit of detail about your personal or employment history. Rather, opt for a simple pitch where you keep things compelling and concise to show exactly why you are the person fit for the job.

Start off by highlighting some of your specific experiences or accomplishments that you are keen to let the interviewer know about before wrapping up the talk about how this prior experience has allowed you to get into a better position for the specific role.

How did you come to know about this position?

This is another one of those innocuous interview questions but it really gives you the opportunity to stand out and show how passionate you are about getting connected to the organization. If it was through a professional contact or friend, specifically name that person before sharing what it was that made things so exciting for you.

If you made the discovery through an article or event posting, remember to share that also. Even if it was through merely a listing on a random job board share the specific aspect that caught your attention regarding that job opening.

What can you tell us about the company?

Reading and reiterating whatever is listed on the "About Us" page of the company does not require a great deal of effort. By asking this question, an interviewer is not really interested in finding out if you understand what the mission is all about but more whether you share these same values and if you are capable of applying it through your own life.

Start with the one line that highlights how much you understand the basic goal of the company. You can do this with the help of a few key phrases and words taken from their website but always remember to switch over to something personal towards the end. Say something like "I really believe in this approach because..." or "I'm personally drawn to this mission because..." and conclude by sharing a couple of examples.

What makes you want to take on this job?

Companies will only hire people who are extremely passionate about their jobs, so the answer to this question as to why you want to apply for this position should ideally be a great one. If you are unable to think of something suitable, it is best that you look elsewhere for openings – because even if you do get the job, you might end up miserable because you can't find a single thing you like about it.

Start by identifying key factors that allow this role to be the perfect fit for you. For example, you can say "I love customer support because I love the constant human interaction and the satisfaction that comes from helping someone solve a problem."

Then, go on to share what makes you love the company so much. You can talk about a common value or principle that you and the company share. For example, you can say, "I've always been very passionate about education. I think you guys are doing great things in this area and I want to help you take it even further."

Why should we hire you?

This may seem like a straightforward question but is also usually the most intimidating one. Nevertheless, consider yourself lucky if you are asked this question as you won't be getting a better opportunity of selling yourself along with your skills to the hiring manager.

You need to come up with an answer that shows three things: you are not only capable of doing the work but you can deliver wonderful results; you will be able to fit in seamlessly with the team and its culture; and you will be a better hire than most of the other potential candidates.

What are your greatest professional strengths?

While answering this question, try to be as accurate as you possibly can. Share the strengths that are true to yourself rather than reflecting upon the things that you feel will be of interest to the interviewer. These should also be relevant and most in line with the position in question.

You also need to be specific – do not just say "people skills" when "relationship building" or "persuasive communication" would sound more appropriate. Remember to follow up with a couple of examples on how you have succeeded in demonstrating these attributes in a professional capacity.

What do you think is your biggest weakness?

More than merely identifying if there are any red-flags to your personality, what your interviewer wants to know by asking this question is to see if you are honest and self-aware. You can't just say "I can''t meet a deadline to save my life" because that is obviously a very negative trait no matter what industry you are in. Saying something such as "I don't think I have any weaknesses" is also not recommended.

Find something that you may be weak at, but you are working on to improve at the moment. For example, you could say that public speaking was never your forte, but you have recently been volunteering to organize events and meetings to help you improve your skills. This shows that you are aware of your weakness and that you are proactively trying to improve upon them.

What is your greatest professional achievement?

The best way to put that "hire me" tag on your forehead is to showcase your track record of having achieved amazing results in your previous jobs. Don't shy away from giving a fitting answer to this question when asked in an interview.

First, describe the task and situation you were required to complete so that the interview has some background context. Then, describe the things that you did to address the situation (action) and the outcome of having done so (result).

A good example would be something along the lines of "In my last job as a junior analyst, it was my role to manage the invoicing process. In one month, I streamlined the process which saved my group 10 man-hours every month and reduced errors on invoices by 25%."

Describe a conflict or challenge that you had encountered at work and what you did to deal with it.

The main purpose of asking this question is to try and determine what your response will be when you're faced with a situation of conflict. A job interview is always the time when people show themselves to be pleasant and nice but nobody knows what will happen once you get into a disagreement with someone from your team or another department.

Describe in detail the specific conflict or challenge, including background context. For example, a coworker from another department may have started deliberately ignoring your emails after his advice on a matter was not followed. Talk about the things that you did to productively and professionally handle the situation. The ending should ideally be a happy one, but even it was not, a potential employer can still learn a lot based on what you did to come up with a compromise or resolution.

Where do you see yourself in five years?

If you happen to be presented with this question, be specific and honest about the goals you have for the future. However, you must take into consideration that a hiring manager will always be interested in knowing a) if you have any realistic goals for your career, b) if you are driven by any particular ambition, c) if the position is in keeping with your growth path and goals, and d) if you are likely to stick around long term as a member of the organization or if you are simply using it as a stopgap while you try to achieve your real goals.

Your best option is to be realistic with the thought process as to where you can end up with this position and give an answer that is along these lines. If you find yourself struggling to come up with a solution, say that you are not sure about what the future has in store for you, but that you are aware of the importance experience will play in helping you take a final stance on the eventual decision.

What is your idea of a dream job?

Once again, the interviewer is interested in trying to figure out if the position really suits your eventual career goals. Saying that "an NBA star" may elicit a few laughs but it will not get you anywhere. The interviewer is looking for anything to positively differentiate you from other candidates, and unless you are interviewing for a spot on a professional or college basketball roster, it is probably better to highlight your ambitions and goals that more closely resonate with the job you are applying for. End by saying how the particular job will take you a step closer to your ambitions.

What other companies are you interviewing with?

There are a number of reasons why you may be asked this question. Sometimes an interviewer asks this in an attempt to determine if you are really serious about working in that particular industry. The question may also be a way to see if you are in demand with several other companies, or if you have simply applied to this one company because you truly feel that you are a perfect fit with them.

The best approach here is ideally to make a mention of how you are looking at a number of similar options in the respective industry that the company deals in. Mentioning that a common characteristic of all the jobs you are looking at require some amount of your skills and critical abilities can turn out to be a major advantage.

A possible answer would be to say, "I am applying for several positions with IT consulting firms where I can analyze client processes and help them to better improve their accounting and bookkeeping practices."

Why are you leaving your current job?

This is one of the tougher questions to answer, and if you are employed at the time you apply for the job you will very likely be asked this question. Let me remind you once again that you need keep the answer a positive one for there can be no gain on your part if you choose to say negative things about your previous employers.

It is better to frame the statement in a way that shows your eagerness to take on new roles and opportunities, such as the one for which you are appearing in the interview. You can talk about how this potential new job is a better fit for your skill set and experience, and that you are excited because of the new role, responsibilities, and opportunities.

For example, you can say, "In my current job, I work in marketing but only from a data analysis standpoint. This new job allows me to do that while also giving me a chance to also work on the creative aspects of marketing, which is something that I am very passionate and excited about."

What got you fired?

In case you are presented the tough follow-up question regarding why you had been let go by a previous employer, and the truth is not the prettiest one to be shared, it is best that you remain honest.

After all, the job-seeking world is a very small one!

However, nobody has asked you to put in a deal-breaker here. Share some of the things that you have done to grow and learn from the experience. Talk about how your approach to life and your career has changed because of that. Show that you have emerged from the experience with a new outlook, more knowledge, and a better work ethic.

What are you looking for in a new position?

Ideally you should bring up the same points that are on offer from this job opening in the organization. It is also advisable that you be specific about your statement. You can say that you are looking for positions that allow you to maximize your skills and experience while also giving you the chance to learn through an increased role and set of responsibilities.

Describe a time that you exercised leadership.

Leadership is a very critical trait that interviewers look for in potential hires, especially if you are applying for a management position. You need to choose an example that does justice to your project management skills and ability to motivate and work with team members. You may have juggled multiple moving parts or spearheaded a project right from the start till the very end. It could also be the ability to effectively and confidently rally a team to meet a deadline that had been deemed impossible.

Remember an important statement while doing so: "The best stories always come with enough detail so as to be memorable and believable." Show the interviewer what you did to engage your leadership skills in such a situation and how it is a representation of your overall leadership potential and experience.

What is that one time when you disagreed with a decision that was made at work?

There are always moments when people end up disagreeing with their bosses. By asking this question to you during an interview, the hiring manager wishes to establish if you are capable of doing so in a professional and productive manner.

It is not a good idea to mention the moment when you had a disagreement with your boss but then decided to give in because he was being a complete jerk and you did not want to upset the peace. It also goes without saying that you should not share a story in which you disagreed with your boss and then continued to do so by refusing to follow orders and choosing to go in a different direction.

Rather, highlight that one scenario where you made a positive difference on the outcome, whether or not you agreed with the method. This could mean a scenario where you respectfully expressed your opinion regarding the matter, but at the same time dutifully followed whatever decision your boss made. It could also be a scenario where you were able to suggest a compromise that would be favorable for everyone involved.

Why did you have a gap in your employment?

If there was a significant period during which you had remained unemployed, be concise and to-the-point about what you had been doing during that time. Highlight things that you did in order to learn new things and improve yourself.

You may have taken up numerous voluntary activities or joined mind-enriching ventures such as taking academic classes or going for blogging. Steer the conversation back towards how you intend to do the job and be a valuable contributor to the organization.

Say things like, "I decided to take a break at the time so that I could focus on self-improvement and mastering new skills, and now I feel that it is time to put everything I have learned into practice by taking on this new role."

Can you explain why you changed career paths?

Changing career paths can be difficult to explain to anyone, let alone a hiring manager. What matters is how you show that the skills and experience you currently possess will help you thrive in your new career.

Put in a few examples to show how you can make the most of your past experience in the new opening you are interviewing for. It is not necessary that you need to make this a direct connection. Sometimes it is more impressive when a candidate is able to put across seemingly irrelevant experiences as extremely relevant ones for the job role in question.

How would your boss and co-workers describe you?

It is important to remember that honesty is the best policy when answering this question. In the event that you get hired, the recruiting manager will be putting through calls to all your former colleagues and bosses, so creating wild, exaggerated stories will not help you when everything is said and done.

Think of all the positive traits that your current manager or other colleagues have complemented you on. Try to highlight some of your traits and strengths that you had not touched upon at any point before in the interview such as your willingness to contribute to other projects when necessary or the kind of strong work ethic that you possess.

It could be other lesser-noticed but nevertheless important positive traits, such as an ability to create well-written e-mails, or the ability to easily put new clients at ease during face-to-face meetings. If you can't think of a single one, then maybe you should consider taking a long, hard look at yourself to see how you can improve and become a better employee!

Chapter 21: Practic Makes Perfect

When I was in school, I took a public speaking class where we had to stand in front of the class and give a five-minute persuasive presentation on a controversial subject. I thought I was prepared enough and that I had enough evidence to persuade my classmates' opinions to align with my own. I had pictures, a heartbreaking story and shocking statistics, but failed to practice before I presented. I figured the subject was shocking enough that I would be able to fill my allotted time with all the information I had found and would just wing the rest of the presentation. I ended up with a presentation of about three minutes, blank stares on my classmates' faces and a less compelling argument than I thought I had. Needless to say, it wasn't my finest moment.

As with any performance or competition, you want to make sure your craft is rehearsed before you are in the spotlight with all eyes on you. You want to deliver a flawless performance, showing that you are prepared and confident. The interviewer is sitting through a few interviews per day, asking the same questions multiple times, and most likely getting many of the same answers. Be that refreshing breath of air that captures their attention from the beginning with your confident smile, firm handshake and appropriate outfit. Then, make them remember you with your convincing answers and captivating personality.

Someone Else's Story

You don't want to be the broken record that the hiring manager has heard too many times before. Try to imagine what the most popular answer might be, then improve on it, or change your answer altogether. Sometimes, the common answers are popular because they are acceptable and agreeable. However, if common answers become too favored by potential hires, then it can appear that the interviewees took the easy way out. Not only will the interviewer have heard the same answers before, but they will be bored with your robotic answers as well as turned off by the lack of creativity. If the open position has opportunities for advancement or managerial elements, the company is most likely looking for a person with leadership qualities who will think and speak for themselves.

Try to give intelligent answers that reflect your preparedness for the interview. There is a difference between sounding rehearsed and sounding prepared so practice with a friend, family member, or even in the mirror. Practice until you are comfortable with your answers.

Mirror, Mirror

I'm an avid mirror-talker. I like to sit in front of my own reflection and see what I look like when I make different expressions or reactions. Often when putting on makeup in the mornings, my husband will catch me playing with my expressions or talking to myself about nothing at all (and sometimes in different accents). Become comfortable with yourself and know what you look like, and how you sound. Work on your voice inflection and volume. Be goofy with your reflection, even if others are watching. The more comfortable you become in your own awkwardness, the more comfortable you'll be in other environments and situations.

If you are struggling with talking to yourself in the mirror to study your expressions and reactions, try starting with something a bit simpler. Put on your favorite song and lip sync along. Pretend you are performing on stage in front of a huge crowd and let them know you're passionate about the lyrics. It's okay to be goofy—in fact, it's recommended! Again, become comfortable in your own skin, building confidence that will emote throughout your interviews.

It sounds like a lot to think about for a little interview, but the following exercises will help you beyond the workplace. They will help you to be more assertive and confident in business and personal relationships.

Expression

When I was very young, my dad would play a game with my sisters and me called 'faces.' He would yell out an expression and we'd have to make that face. "Happy Face!" and we'd plaster the biggest smiles on our faces showing every one of our teeth. "Angry Face!" and we'd furrow our brows, scrunch our noses and purse our lips while tucking our chins down to our chests.

Though it was a child's game helping us to develop and express our emotions, the game is wonderful when practicing for interviews. Given your actual expressions and reactions will be more subtle, the same idea stands. Watch to see how you react to information, whether it is exciting or cautionary. You might be amazed at how your reactions do not come across in regular conversation as much as you think they do (or, contrary wise, come across too strong). I have interviewed so many people who seemed like they were just staring right through me the entire time. They looked completely vacant; though I'm sure they thought they were engaging in the conversation. Remember that a blank face or minimal facial expressions can read as bored or uninterested. Who wants to hire someone that isn't interested or passionate about the position and company?

Voice Inflection, Volume and Pronunciation

It is so important to be heard. Not only should you speak up, but you also want to articulate your words so that you can be perfectly understood. We've all experienced trying to talk with someone that mumbles his or her words. Either you are stuck asking 'what?' after each statement, or you give up and nod, pretending like you know what is being said, looking for a way out of the conversation. Along with being aware of your expression, you want to consciously adjust your vocal inflection.

I have endured many interviewees who spoke in such dreadful monotone it bored me to hear their answers. Particularly, the position I was looking to hire for was one with a high level of customer service.

There was no way I would allow anyone who spoke in a monotone during the interview to talk to my clients. I'd lose business!

As you focus on your voice inflection, play with the different levels of your voice. Of course, you won't want to fluctuate too much when being interviewed, sounding like a child's cartoon, but you certainly do not want to stay at one even tone the entire time. By playing with the levels of inflection in your voice, you will be able to place emphasis on the important points you want to make within your interview while letting your interviewer know that you are involved in the conversation.

Volume and inflection go hand in hand. In regular conversation, you will notice that more often than not, we tend to drop the ends of our sentences. We were taught in grade school that when we come to the end of a sentence we drop our voices to signify the period. The problem with this rule in interviews is that oftentimes, we'll mumble the ends of our sentences, making our sentence conclusion unclear.

Likewise, we were taught to raise our vocal pitch when asking questions to denote the question mark.

Now to shake up everything you've learned---try to raise your pitch slightly when coming to the end of a sentence and speak out.

This doesn't mean to make the sentence into a question, but rather ditch the mumbled ending as follows:

I worked there for four years.

You can still present an end to your statement, but this way, the end of your answer will not be lost. This is a great exercise to practice either with a friend or by recording yourself. Find any magazine, book or pamphlet, and read a page while trying to raise your pitch to create a strong finish to your sentences. You'll be able to hear a clear difference.

Nervous Ticks

Everyone has his or her own nervous ticks. A nervous tick is anything that you do subconsciously to keep your nerves at bay or to stay focused. The only downfall is that these ticks are repeated physical actions that clearly signify that the nerves are present. Sometimes we develop these ticks to delay answering or to find the right words to say, but it only distracts from your actual answers.

My own nervous tick was throwing in "uhh" in my sentences. At first, I had no idea how many times I would interrupt my idea. After recording myself, I was surprised at how unpleasant that sound would make my answers. Instead of hearing what I was saying on the recording, I was distracted by how many times the "uhh" came into my speech. My problem was that my brain worked much faster than I could speak, and I would either end up stumbling over my words, or creating a space to slow down and articulate. To remedy this tick, I worked on slowing down my answers, consciously choosing my words and avoiding any space fillers.

Other common ticks include things like clearing your throat before each answer, constantly playing with your hair, certain repeated hand gestures, space fillers ("umm"/"uhh"), leg bouncing, touching your face, rubbing your hands on your legs, and many more. Be aware of these types of ticks in yourself that may distract from your interview.

The Minute You Walk Through the Door

The minute you open that office door, the interview has begun (and a quick hint - that designated minute better be before the scheduled time for the interview). 'Being on time' means that you are checking in with the receptionist about five to ten minutes prior to your allotted interview appointment. This shows characteristics of time management and responsibility. Don't let your interviewer wait on you. To be on time, there are a few things to consider when preparing for your interview: Set your alarm to wake you nice and early so you have time to get ready and double check all your interview supplies. Look up the directions to the interviewer's office the night before. Check the traffic report to allow for enough driving time.

Let's face it. Life happens. If something happens that puts you behind schedule to the point where you know you won't make the interview on time, call ahead and quickly explain your situation and location. It is better that your interviewer knows you are going to be later than expected than to think you are just bad with time management.

Be cordial with anyone at the reception desk, be pleasant, and even smile at anyone who happens to walk by while you wait to be interviewed. You never know who your immediate supervisor will be once you get the job, so it's better to start work relationships in a very professional manner. One of my bosses made sure to be in his office with the door closed when the candidates would come in to interview. He would have me sit at the front desk and get a feel for the person while they were waiting for him. Little did they know they were already being interviewed and examined by me. I look much younger than my age, which made me less threatening to engage in a conversation. No one suspected that I had any say in the hiring process.

One woman that was coming to interview was told that she would be speaking with my boss, a man. She arrived dressed in tight, revealing clothing, hair teased and curled, and thick red lipstick. She walked up to me and asked me to "let him know I'm here, hun." I couldn't believe it. She then proceeded to fluff her hair and position her…assets…while waiting for my boss. It sounds like something out of a bad movie, but, alas, I've seen it all. Needless to say, she did not get the job.

If you get that position, you're going to be working closely with all the employees in the office. You'll be spending so much time with these people, and they all deserve your upmost respect. Every one of those employees will have a different personality. There are different personality types that are wonderfully suited for specific jobs and your success will be, in part, how you can thrive while working with ALL types of personalities. If nothing else, show your (future) co-workers respect as you are all working towards a common goal.

Let Me Hear Your Body Talk

Even if the words from your mouth are intelligent and absorbing, what is your body language saying? With the wrong body language, you could be sending opposing messages to your interviewer.

I was interviewing a candidate who was perfect on paper and even showed up to the interview dressed to impress. He successfully engaged me with his answers, and impressed me with his knowledge of the company, but there was one thing that hindered his chances of getting the position: his body language. This candidate slouched in the chair, put his foot up on the coffee table, avoided making eye contact and even interrupted my questions to provide his answers. His body language told me he wasn't interested in speaking to me and his know-it-all demeanor came off as rude and arrogant.

He had become too comfortable with the routine of interviewing. He did everything right to prepare himself for the questions of the interview, but forgot to maintain his professional presence. He acted as though I was wasting his time by asking him the same questions that other potential employers had asked him in past interviews. Even if this was the umpteenth time he interviewed, he should have treated it like his first and only.

Be aware of your body language and stature. Sit up straight, make eye-contact with your interviewer and show them your most professional self while engaging them in conversation. Nod in agreement when listening to the interviewer explain the position and skill requirements and ask questions when you are unsure what they are talking about. Let your body talk just as loudly as your voice.

If this particular candidate had cared to pay attention to my body language, he would have recognized my discomfort with his disposition and my dissipating interest in him as an employee.

Conclusion

Thank you again for taking the time out to read this. I hope that you found value in what I had to say and gained some perspective of what we think about during the hiring process. I am terrible at writing formal advice in a text book format because the bull shit that they write about will only take you so far. I like to use the 80/20 rule in almost every aspect of my life. 20% of your daily actions will give you 80% of your results. I put the 20% of what matters during the interview process into this book and saved you time, money, and effort by excluding all of the bull shit you see in so many interviewing guides. The fact of the matter is, the more engaging, detail oriented, and genuinely interested you are in the position, the better you chances are of getting the job. In parting I have some final thoughts to send you with and wish you all the success you deserve.

From this day forward take further initiative in your life to get better at what you do and what you want to do.

Take care of yourself. Go get exercise in any way that interests you. You will be happier and become more interesting as you become more vibrant. Successful people are full of energy and exercise plays a huge role in that.

Read daily. The more you read, the more you can learn. More importantly, your ability to communicate with others will slowly get better over time and become better than 90% of your competition. Most people hate reading so it is such an easy way to start standing out.

Stop worrying so much. Life is beautiful because it is precious and finite. Each and every day we wake up is the only morning we are promised. Take full advantage and focus on being happy.

Want to stand out from others? Smile at them. Most people walk around with a miserable look on their faces. People like happy, approachable people. Find every opportunity to smile at someone.

Show a genuine interest in others and they will link pleasure to the value you bring them. Listeners are hard to come by and everyone wants to be heard. Be a good listener.

Run toward opportunities to get better. "If you are being challenged, you are growing."

Approach life as if it is a big game and success is just a way to keep score. Go home at night happy, knowing you can go back at it and compete again tomorrow.

www.ingramcontent.com/pod-product-compliance
Lightning Source LLC
Chambersburg PA
CBHW072009070526
44583CB00015B/1400